Mrs. Shruti Prabhakar

First Published in March 2022

ISBN: 978-93-5472-922-5

BLUEROSE PUBLISHERS
www.BlueRoseONE.com
info@bluerosepublishers.com
+91 8882 898 898

Cover Design:
Aveek

Typographic Design:
Rohit

Distributed by: BlueRose, Amazon, Flipkart

BABA NAAM KEVALAM

Your Life Was A Blessing
Your Memory Is A Treasure
You Are Loved Beyond Words
And Missed Beyond Measure.

Love You Aarushi

Hello Friends

I have dedicated this book to my daughter Aarushi Prabhakar. The idea of writing this book sprouted when she left me alone in this world. Her story and struggles were something that I wanted the people to know. This book was very emotional for me to write. I want to thank Aarushi for coming into my life and inspiring me to write this book. Two of us shared an extraordinary bond, which is visible in our relationship. She was a real fighter, a gem kind of personality who had determination, commitment, toughness, talent, and whatnot. I feel blessed to be called her Mom. Thank you, Arshu.

I want to thank Baba (My guru), whom I think has chosen me to do this fantastic job of writing this book under his guidance.

A special thanks to my husband (Aakash Prabhakar), without whom this dream of mine would not have been possible. He never stopped me from chasing my dreams. I appreciate your care and support all the time. You are always there throughout the ups and downs of life; thank you for being my rock.

I have heartfelt gratitude to my dear brother Ritish, my son Shouryan, my friends, and most importantly, my family members who stood by my side and tolerated each step with me.

Many thanks to Samiksha Singh for contributing to the book and making it a smooth read.

Thank you to the entire team of Blue Rose Publication, who made this happen.

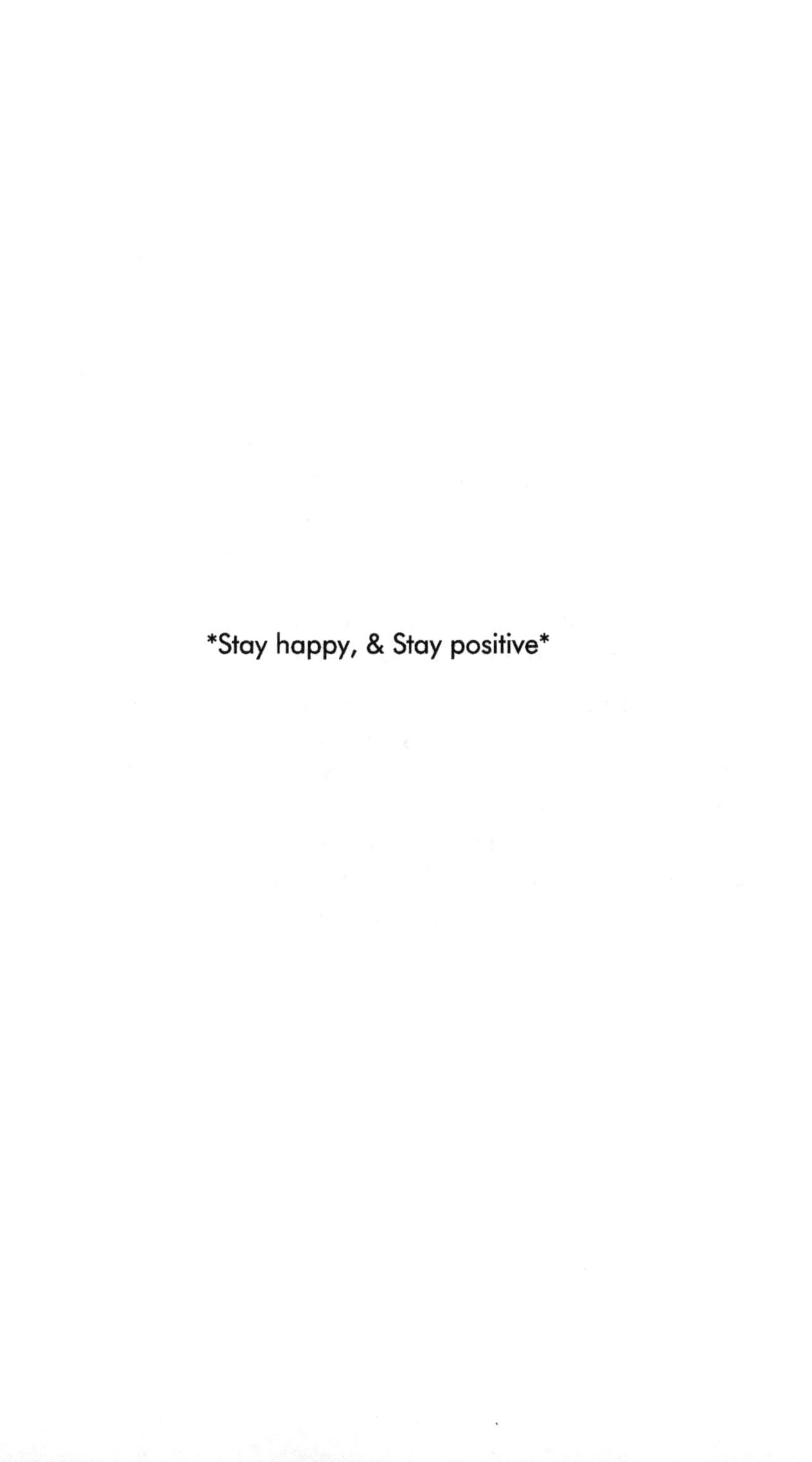

Stay happy, & Stay positive

Introduction

I, Shruti Prabhakar, grew up in Punjab (Jalandhar). Being one from a middle-class family, I always dreamed of doing something that could make my family proud of me. I graduated from Guru Nanak Dev University, Amritsar, and post-graduation from Himachal Pradesh University, Shimla. I had a passion for becoming a teacher. Where I am currently working, I thought I would be! a teacher in one of the renowned Schools of Dehradun (St. Jude's School). Traveling, reading books, and of course, looking after my family in the best possible way is my hobby.

Nothing brings me more contentment than seeing my kids in front of my eyes. I always just wished to get the best out of my children. And I can proudly say that I am hundred percent successful in doing so. And if I talk about my personality, then I am someone who would also love to be a good listener, which always made me understand the current or might happen situations.

Contents

CHAPTER ONE

Zindagi

ज़िन्दगी!

ज़िन्दगी!
दो पल की है ये जिन्दगी,
इसको तू हँसी से जी ले!
मत बता अपने दुख के अफसाने,
इसको तू अमृत समझ के पी ले!

लम्हों को तू जी,
जैसे ये न आयेंगे दोबारा!
अपने दुखों को भुलाकर,
खुशी को बनाले सहारा!

जिन्दगी देगी ठोकरें,
तू गिर तू उठ!
वो आंसू जो उस पल बहेंगे,
तेरे अपनो की खुशी
बयां करेगी, उनका सुख!

जो तूने आज है खोया,
एक दिन तू वापिस पायेगा उसे!
आज ज़िन्दगी का साथ दे,
ज़िन्दगी निराश नहीं करेगी तुझे!

AARUSHI PRABHAKAR
30th APRIL 2020

[Meaning]

Life is an award from time,
Accept life with all its moments.
Some happy and some not,
For every rose that has a thorn,
Fragrance and prick,
Accept both.
Enjoy and endure equally,
And smile.
For it is just a one-time award.
A grant, a bliss, a gift.
Embrace it in all its aspects,
Smile!

'I Am Gonna Make The Rest Of My Life

The Best Of My Life'

Life is a series of different episodes through which every person goes. Experiencing different situations, events, and phases. God has never been partial to anyone while writing about one's destiny. Everyone is born with a different destiny; created by the supreme being. The person who truly understands that life is a blend of negatives and positives, and that gloom in life doesn't last for a lifetime, is the one who can win over the phases of feeling lost and depressed.

I am 18 years old but have gone through a lot of trouble and health-related issues. I am not telling this to gain any sympathy but just to make my feelings clear. I don't think for even a single year, I have lived a normal routine life like any other child of my age.

Life is not easy! Life means: -

1. Bad days
2. Good days

3. Sorrows
4. Happiness
5. Success
6. Failures

The best way to improve your life is to practice what you have learned in the days of frustration as well as the hard days! Get yourself close to a person who proves to be the best inspiration for you. Feel positive at all times. There is just one mantra that can help you to overcome your hard days, that is, "EVERYTHING WAS ALRIGHT, EVERYTHING IS ALRIGHT AND EVERYTHING WILL BE ALRIGHT" and you can face any thunder coming your way.

Truly speaking, for me the biggest inspiration is myself. I know, I am the girl who would never give up, who would face any situation, and will come up again with more strength. This is life!! Know yourself first, your capabilities and then live life to the fullest.

If God takes away one thing from you, he shall gift you another blessing. For me, the blessing is the kind of person I am. I found my inner self during my school life. I was very active during my school days. A debater, a dancer, an actress, a hostess, and a planner. I found the will to work hard and do what I feel is right, and I will be appreciated. I know I am confident, competent and most importantly, capable. Bad days should not hinder your life's good times or interfere in your career!

Be thankful for what you are today. The whole world is suffering more than you or me. I remember a girl who used to be a runner; she lost her legs in a terrible accident and was suggested by many to end her career as a runner. But she never gave up. She had willpower and strength and believe it or not, she climbed Mount Everest with her prosthetic legs. I mean wow! Such willpower and confidence are required in life which let you explore more of what you are and what you can do. She is truly an inspiration for many!

Have a perspective in your life. Life is good and discomfort is temporary. Don't get frightened to enter in this discomfort! Face it fearlessly and let it strengthen you.

I would end my article with some beautiful lines by Henry Wordsworth,

"LIFE IS REAL! LIFE IS EARNEST! AND THE GRAVE IS NOT ITS GOAL DUST THOU ART, TO DUST THOU RETURNEST, WAS NOT SPOKEN OF THE SOUL"

These beautiful lines are not mine but my daughter's. She always believed that life should be filled to the brim and I always feel awestruck after reading every single word. Providing meanings, a perception, a path but how did she do it! She is someone who just does not want to explore every second of her life but wants to create a moment, a lesson, a solution to the questions out of it. Like she said in her article.

I know you all must be thinking, what is so special about her or any of her stories that a mother wants to convey, but every story has its reality which sets it apart.

'Pages after pages all will make sense.'

LIFE SPENT WELL

I was sitting beside that tree,
With some bread and a cup of tea.
Waiting for an opportunity to come,
To get a diary in my hand and call my mum.

I just want us to sit together,
And write our destination.
So that, at the end of this play of life,
We have no complaints but satisfaction.

God please, give me a day,
To write my miseries and to pray.
Let there be no tear,
But a life filled with joy, without any fear.

I just want a life spent well,
So that when I grow old,
I have these memories to carry me away,
How beautiful my life is, I would say!

-AARUSHI
29 /2/16

Every line screamed how she wanted to let her imagination wear wings of her dreams to become the reality of her life.

I had that rage in me sometimes earlier, that after being such a bright child, filled with all the innocence of the world, I ask why her? Why was she not given the normality every other person had? Why does she have to even think of just living a day with a normal routine instead of having one? Why does every ounce of air she breathes make her realize it is way more precious, that it shouldn't be wasted? But she never thought the way I did. Even in those difficulties where she couldn't even have a bite of food, where any other normal person, including myself, felt lifeless; she still managed to be filled with vivacity to participate in her daily challenges which were being plotted due to her illness. As time went by, she became my source of energy to let myself watch her going through the pain. She explained, 'Mother, happiness in life should not become an option and it should stay with you every possible time as discomfort is temporary just like the darkness.'

I had to agree with her thoughts but couldn't help myself but asked 'Okay, so you only tell me what is happiness in life?' Then here she goes,

HAPPINESS IN LIFE

I will not cry,
I will let my cheeks dry,
Life is full of lightning and thunder,
Many pirates are ready to plunder.

But if I see my life with calmness,
I think that it can be decorated with happiness.
Enthusiastic life is a good one and experience full too,
But it can be made if you don't have the sad flu.

So, forget the past and don't think of the future,
Make your present your life's best feature.
Work like an ant and enjoy like a free bird!
Tension only at the workplace and be happy with your beloved!!

-AARUSHI PRABHAKAR

23/11/16

And after this explanation, I was speechless.

CHAPTER TWO

The Beginning

The journey of my new life started when I got married on 2nd October 2000, which took place after some strange coincidences. My aunty used to live in Dehradun and I went there to attend my cousin's marriage. It may sound a bit extra like a Bollywood film, but what is a book without an extraordinary tale? So, apparently my husband saw my photograph in the album of my cousin's marriage.

Later, when the marriage proposal reached my father, he started charming me up about the details regarding my to be husband and guess what? I didn't want to say yes to the marriage because of the distance, as it was far-flung from my hometown. So when my family was traveling to meet the boy all the way to his place in Dehradun, I was continuously praying for the rejection of this marriage proposal. It was funny to acknowledge the time when my mind didn't want to stay far from my parents but I had no other option other than listening to my parent's advice. Especially my father's words, because neither I was frank enough to express my hard feelings nor I wanted to deny their decision because, at the end of the day, I knew and also had this feeling in me that they are my parents. Every decision for my life taken by them will be beneficial for me and it will be the right thing to do.

There is another fun fact. After finalizing the marriage, everyone decided to commence the engagement ceremony the next morning itself, when my in-laws were supposed to visit my aunt's house in Dehradun along with my husband. Until that time, I didn't even see him once, not even his photograph. I know it's tough to digest in this era but at that time I took a step towards the new beginning of my life with a blindfold over my eyes.

Finally, we started talking to each other. 3 months after the engagement I had to talk to him as it was his birthday. And post that, we started the trend of being the love birds in the family. We used to write letters to each other. No doubt saying that it was indeed romantic. With every letter, there used to be a card with heartfelt lines and every other week we exchanged letters, all until our marriage. The letters made me fall for him. We became so close in those months, that at my in-laws everyone made assumptions after seeing our bond that it's a love marriage.

Immediately after my marriage, I conceived my first child about whom I got to know in and around mid-November but due to some issues, the child couldn't survive for more than a month in my womb. In late December, I had a miscarriage. And we all know how a miscarriage affects the mother. So, I was perturbed but my husband really gathered me emotionally as well as supported me by quoting, 'It happens sometimes, you don't have to worry about anything. We have a lot of time and it's just the beginning.'

At that point, I was in my final year of M.Com in Himachal Pradesh University, and of course, the miracle occurred when we least expected it. My miracle happened in the same way, when I got the news that I am expecting again in the month of April, 2001. And as I had the miscarriage before, we didn't want to be incautious regarding anything. So we were more meticulous.

We lived our lives to the fullest in those nine months. We were happy to the core and there was not a single Sunday where we didn't go for an outing. My mother-in-law also used to comment that 'You roam this much, I am afraid that your baby might be born in the car itself'. And everytime, we would have a big laugh. I cannot forget the time when my baby was growing every day inside me, I was about to give birth to a new life. It's true that other than a mother, no one else can understand the beauty of it, because those feelings are unfeasible to put out into words.

In every possible manner, I used to feed my body and mind with happiness so that my baby would come into this life with all the happiness and positivity. It was the fun part but there were times when I didn't want anyone near me too. The food made me lose it with the smell, 'yellow pulses' to be precise where I used to feel puckish most of the time. Yes, you know right! It was nothing but morning sickness which actually has the capacity to make your life a living hell. And in the first week of December, I went to my mother's house. We did plan it earlier that it was the first child so we should go to Punjab for the firstborn.

CHAPTER THREE

Mere Ghar Aayi Ek Nanhi Pari

Heartiest congratulations on the birth of Laxmi. My world changed in a split second when my little angel, the princess of my life, took birth on 30th December 2001 at 5:00 in the morning. And how can I forget about the night before when my body was experiencing insufferable pain, while I was going under the forceps delivery. My mind had some anonymous dense clouds of selfdoubt. Like I won't even think of having a second child and guess what? I did share this thought with my mother too but she would only know the feeling of being a mother. That is why she asked me to stop filling my mind with cynicism. The exertion was real and after some time, I got shifted to the OT at around 4:15 am. My mother had been told by the doctors about the complication coming ahead in the normal delivery because the head of the baby was bigger than usual. Hence, they might have to opt for cesarean but somehow it worked out in the end with forceps. I wasn't fond of believing in miracles but as soon as the doctor held my little life and kept her over my stomach, the words would be less to express my blissful feelings. And from there on I did start to believe in miracles.

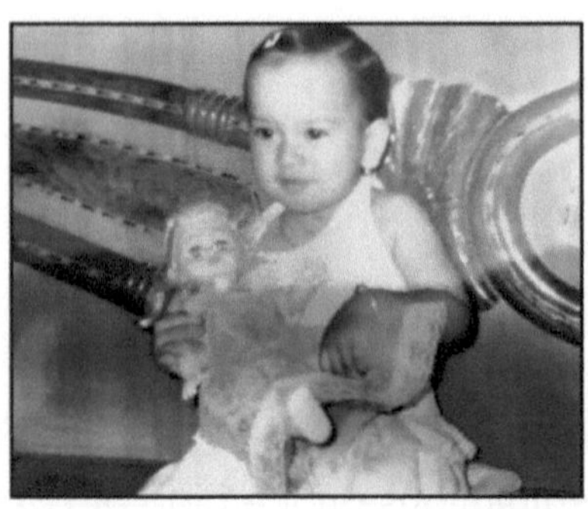

Look at this beauty and how angelic she looks!

I was touched like nothing else by the feeling that nothing is as beautiful as giving birth to a child. I would say how blessed we ladies are, that Gods have given us the strength to bring a life into this world. I was remarkably happy to see and feel my newborn over my stomach, I wasn't even aware whether it was a girl or a boy.

The doctors gave me anesthesia for the stitches and I was in deep sleep. I don't remember exactly, the moment I came back to my senses where I saw my mother sitting on the opposite side of the bed, holding my baby in her hands. I asked her what it was? Jokingly she answered, "Go back to sleep, it's a girl".

My happiness knew no bounds the time my ears heard those words from my mother. Excitedly, I told my mother 'Very good. This is what I wanted', and of course, I took a decision to try and dispense every happiness to my daughter as well as raise her just like people raise their sons.

My in-laws are settled in Dehradun so in the meantime my father rang my husband and told him "Aakashji, Laxmi Aayi Hai".

Aakash was totally thrilled after listening to the gleeful news. He came to Jalandhar by evening and by the time

I was shifted back to home,I still remember the twinkle in his eyes when he held our little angel for the first time. He was not just happy but was also feeling the calmness and warmth while holding our daughter, which I could see on his face. She was like an angel. When she took birth, light-hued, red hands like someone have put blush and chubby too.

My younger brother Ritish was in 6th std and he used to walk around the whole house holding his little niece in his hands. As soon as he was back home from school, he simply used to throw his bag in the corner and come straight to the baby to share lots of kisses. He did make her cheeks all red by sharing kisses on the cheeks, her forehead, on her little hands, and so on. It really felt like all of us were after the one beautiful angel.

On the very first night, that is the night 30th Dec 2001, my husband didn't allow my mother to sleep next to our baby, he said 'You all take rest, I will take care of her' and the whole night, Aakash was awake to take care of our angel. He never hesitated to change her diapers. There was nothing but happiness on his face; he wasn't tired for a single moment after being awake for the night and taking care of our princess. Instead of resting the next morning, Aakash went to buy some beautiful woollen dresses, in which our daughter looked so pretty. There were bundles of clothes. I guess that she hardly repeated her clothes at that time. Aarushi's maternal grandfather used to sing a song specially composed for her to put her to sleep on his chest. Again, I must say she really brought so much joy, love, and happiness in our lives. With her, the days used to feel like hours, hours like minutes, and minutes like seconds. I didn't realize the part of how time is running with her, I wish I had the power to freeze some moments forever.

After coming back to Dehradun from Jalandhar, everyone was thrilled to welcome the little baby. She has been nurtured with all the love and blessings, swinging in the arms of her grandparents. A religious function was held by my in-laws two days after her arrival. My little baby got her name which had to be done by my sister-in-law and she kept a beautiful name for our daughter 'AARUSHI' meaning 'the first rays of the sun, life giving'. And this name wasn't just a name for her identity, but it actually matched her personality in every manner.

Aakash used to sing a song by holding her in his arms and she kept jumping after listening to it. How special the bond between a father and a daughter can be is known by everyone.

For every Sunday she had outings with Aakash. She grew up with this routine. She was in good health, and was fond of soft drinks, apple flavored cereals, fast food and many other things. And by the time she started taking her first steps, right before her first birthday, I remember how happy we were after seeing this. On her first birthday, Aarushi's grandmother arranged for a religious function and after that, we arranged an elegant dinner where the house was filled with tremendous gratification. She looked so beautiful in her pretty dress. She was wearing a frock with a high neck, a belly with socks and the whole look was in the colour white just like Cinderella.

She always used to be healthy, but one day she got really sick. She felt choked due to the cold but in the end, when you have a naughty kid around, it's almost impossible to catch up with their energy level. They get sick and after some time, they are back on their energy to play and run. She also used to walk on her toes; never kept her full feet on the ground and I got to know from my mother that I used to do the same in my childhood. My kid just knew how to live life to the fullest. Even when she was too young to understand the meaning of happiness, she would just smile and after seeing her smiles, our days were filled with full energy to move into the next chapter of her life.

CHAPTER FOUR

A Change

All those days were the best time of my existence that I can imagine. But time doesn't have the property of stagnation as it changes, due to which you always have indecision about one thing, would you get to experience those beautiful episodes back in your life or not? We all live in the aspiration that somewhere or somehow one day, happiness will encounter you on the roads of uncertainty. I know after filling your mind with all those beautiful memories of mine, you all might think why suddenly I am sounding like everything is not perfect!

Actually, you all are thinking right because now I feel like a walking corpse who just knows how to function the body system. My life is nothing now but all changed, because my miracle, my angel, my happiness just left me alone on this earth.

My daughter 'AARUSHI PRABHAKAR IS NO MORE'.

For writing this line and telling you all about the truth of my present life, I had to accumulate an immense amount of bravery which took another few days to write again. My hands are still shivering, my eyes are wet again while writing about reality. Sometimes I just wish that I am dreaming; that my angel will come by walking in my room, standing next to me and waking me up by saying **'Mom wake up, it was just a bad dream'.** Lots of people, including my family, apprise me that one day you have to move on but I just don't know what it means! How could you move on with the fact that a precious part of your life, the reason for your happiness, won't be coming back to you ever. And you have to live with this reality which makes the situation even worse.

People think that, what a nightmare it must be to go through the tough times, but it wasn't the days when we were struggling to make her fine from her disease. For me, it was the days where we had to live without her. The day she stopped breathing, since then our every day and night has been a nightmare. I am not able to remember anything except her. The pain is undeniably killing which can just make you think to stop living for once.

In 2017,

It was the 30th August and the day of utter sadness. Aarushi's last exam in her school had become the genesis of a trail which was embarking her life towards the predicament. Her face was as long as fiddle, she slept off and my thoughts just touched the possibilities of being in exertion as due to last night, she was frazzled enough while doing the concoction. On the eve of that day when she woke up, I entered her room as always, I became acquainted with her ailment as her temperature was raised. I gave her medication while just satisfying my own intellect till night. And for the next three days too, it's nothing more than exertion.

On 2nd September, she had the stipulation as well as the forethought with her father in a matter of going out for a movie. I refused as her health was the first concern but when she insisted and my husband told us that she will be recuperated by stepping out of the house. So we had no other choice rather than accepting his decision to make her feel happy even if she was down with the high temperature. Then, we four, me, my husband, Aarushi and my son reached our destination to watch the movie and the moment Aakash parked the car, she threw up all of a sudden. I again suggested getting back home but Aarushi gave an explanation that it happened because of motion sickness. Then, somehow we went inside as she was stubborn enough. Fifteen minutes later after the interval, she again started to feel a little sick, where she couldn't sit inside the hall anymore. So, finally we decided to go back home as soon as possible.

While we were on the way, she started asking me to not attend school the next morning and when I questioned her about why she was saying so, she just replied 'Mumma I am not feeling good.' I tried to explain to her my situation being an employee at the private school. Also I told her that she won't have to wait for long or stay alone at home because by the time Aakash will leave for his work which used to be 11 am, I will reach home within 1.5 or maybe 2 hours. But she wasn't ready to listen and asked me to arrange for my substitution by making a call to the coordinator. I yelled at her that this can't be done as I just can't take a day off all of a sudden which can lead to some kind of issue at school for me.

A day after it, on 5th September 'Teachers Day' and the number of students was low as the exams had just gotten over. It was raining heavily. I was sitting with my friend with a pessimistic feeling in my head and my friend asked me why I was behaving in a divergent manner. But Aarushi wasn't getting any healthier so my mind kept me away from the work zone. I went to the coordinator in order to inform her that I want to visit my daughter but she said if Aarushi will feel sick or queasy, she will make a call to you. And then you can take a leave and go back to her. After listening to my coordinator's statement, I had to agree as well. And I went back to my friend.

I told her that I wasn't getting any positive vibes, my gut was speaking out loud about the possibility of being right too. I was feeling anxious and at the same time my friends at the school mentioned that it has been years since I have been facing struggles or you can say from the beginning itself there were many ups and downs but they never saw me in this condition that I was facing on that day. Then I rushed to the principal's office to take a leave as I wanted to see my child as soon as possible. I wanted to make sure that she was alright or if she wasn't then what's the reason behind my anxious feelings. I reached her office and told my principal about Aarushi's health as well as the low attendance of my class. I also asked to put a substitution at my position by combining two classes in one as there wasn't just the prostration but a disease which grew enough to take anyone's life.

As soon as I came back to my home from school, I couldn't understand what I should do next when I did not have the car. But all I knew was that I have to take Aarushi for the blood tests and Aakash reviewed that I have the habit of exaggerating things which I wasn't ready to listen to. I did make up my mind to get done with the blood tests but this time without being persuasive for my thoughts with my husband. I thought that once the reports will transpire, everything will be known to us whether I am just hallucinating for her health or is there any real problem which my daughter has to face next!

I took my steps towards Aarushi and asked her to accept my request of taking her to the lab for her blood tests. I was trying to tell her that it won't hurt much, just a little penetration of injection. I was feeling anxious for her health, as it's getting worse with the passing time. So after listening to this, she agreed. As I mentioned already, it was raining heavily so without thinking about wasting one more minute, I made her wear a raincoat and took her to the lab by riding on my scooter. After reaching the lab, I asked the assistant to do all the tests like jaundice, typhoid, etc. to make sure my gut feeling must be unburdened but the assistant insisted not to do any tests as according to him my daughter looked fine. I was not feeling any certainty in that statement. He kept convincing me not to let Aarushi go for the tests or my money will be squandered over or what not! I really couldn't understand how he could be so sure about my daughters' condition or health. But I made sure he conducted all the tests I entered for. I did exactly what I decided earlier when I convinced Aarushi to visit the lab despite such weather.

The time when I got her reports, it was 5 pm. I arrived at the lab even before the expected time after dropping Aarushi home. I found out that there are two positives in the tests, one was Typhoid and the other was Jaundice. The lab assistant asked me that instead of being indecisive as I couldn't be revealed towards the possibilities without seeing the results in real. But how I was assuredly mentioned that something was up with my daughter so I told him, "It's just one of the symptoms of being a mother". I took a deep breath and then I called my cousin who practices in Jalandhar as a gynecologist, to ask what am I supposed to do now after I had the colloquy about the test results. She advised me to take Aarushi to a good physician, not to any child specialist, as she was crossing her adolescence.

I called Aakash right away after the call with my cousin. I told him about the whole situation and asked him to search as I was advised by my cousin. We went to the doctor with all Aarushi's previous medical records. The doctor himself got shocked seeing the long profile of a little girl in the medical history. At that time Aarushi's condition was degrading with every moment, she was laying over my lap like she was unconscious and I even gave a look to my husband to acknowledge her condition but he just said that it's happening only because she is sustaining Jaundice. And there is no need to get nervous as we are already in front of the doctor, she will be fine soon. The doctor then gave her a few medicines which were required immediately. At that point of time Aarushi had 5 or 6 mg/dL level of bilirubin in the blood which is considered as not less but still manageable Jaundice. With the medicines, a strict diet should be maintained like coconut water, green vegetables etc. Also asked us to visit for the checkup after 2 days and we did maintain the equivalency with doctors. But there was no improvement in her health and her condition got even substandard than before.

On the third day, we visited the clinic again for the checkup as we were asked to do so. But the doctor wasn't available at that moment. So, we were directed to his junior in the clinic, as the one who looked upon Aarushi's medical condition two days ago had to go abroad for some work. The junior doctor prescribed the connate artifact which was 'perpetuate with the medication and she will be alright'. I was so confused about the condition my daughter was going into. Because I wasn't aware enough about the Jaundice and again as the time was passing by; things were getting difficult. But we were just hoping to see Aarushi get out of that illness. My parents came from Jalandhar to link up with her.

One day she was just sedentary inside my room and watching the television with us at night, it was 8th of September. I still remember her words when she asked me to hand over my mobile. And the moment I gave her the mobile, she looked with an indignant face towards me and shrieked by saying 'What am I asking from you and what are you handing me over? I asked you to pass me the television remote, not the mobile phone!' After listening to her statement I felt something weird about her deportment but there was more to it. She was holding the monteith and kept rotating it from every four corners, after comprehending her in a course of preternatural action. I kept thinking about what had happened to her! Our bedrooms were on the upper floor and the kitchen, as well as the drawing-room, was on the ground floor. I started crying the moment I came downstairs from the bedroom and my mother followed me too. I raised a query to her that she also noticed Aarushi's behaviour. So, my mother told me that she thought no one else discerned because Aakash and my father were also sitting in the same room but they didn't react.

It wasn't just upsetting but painful for me to watch her doing some eccentric venture due to her extensively increasing health issues. Next day my parents had to go back to Jalandhar where Aarushi also buckled herself to the railway station with me in order to wish 'bon voyage' to her grandparents. While sitting inside the car as the growing weakness couldn't let her acquire enough strength to debouch or walk, she just gesticulated while my parents were leaving. After a day or two, a lady who used to work at my school as a cleaner got me introduced to some different treatment which has been going on for years I guess!

I know it will sound not just different but unintelligent, especially in the era of modern science that I actually lay hold of my daughter to a guy who says that jaundice can be cured if you put patient hands in the mixture of calcium hydroxide and water where the mixture will turn yellow. And by repeating the same process over a few days her Jaundice can be cured. As they believe that when the water is mixed with calcium hydroxide, it pulls out the illness which befall in the Jaundice. But you have to accomplish the citation before the sunset in order to succeed and that's how the water turns yellow which was certifiable to observe or I should say insane to even verbalize something which isn't medically possible. And the guy who performed it, also repeated the same statement that there is nothing to dwell on in essence, it deems grievous because she is too feeble and I actually believed for the moment. If medicine can't help my daughter, maybe this process might work, which is totally insane.

It was Sunday so I asked my husband to accompany me on the next day while I was performing the citation. My husband denied but I pleaded with him to come along as I was feeling anxious again that something is not right! The time we reached that place and while Aakash was helping her to get out of the car, Aarushi vomited in the hands of my husband itself. We both were shocked as we looked towards each other with thought, is this what happens to a Jaundice patient! Then while she was putting her hands in the mixture, I asked the same guy about the thought that was coming before into my mind that this is how a Jaundice patient goes through the illness? Every patient with Jaundice suffers analogously the way my daughter is suffering? So, the guy answered yes, but she is suffering a little more because of the immense weakness.

The silence was on the colossal level like the car was moving by itself. Throughout the way while coming back home, we were quite like we didn't want to talk about anything that was happening with us. Or maybe the truth was we didn't know what to discuss or make a statement about! We reached home and Aakash hauled Aarushi in his arms and took her to the room. We went for the procedure in the morning. When Aakash came downstairs again, we were just sitting like our brain has been iced out, still, no words to say, no food has been made and we didn't even care as our appetite died too. Instantaneously, an ice breaker happened when I suggested to my husband to look for some other doctor and he agreed. While being seated at the same place Aakash placed the call to his friends in order to take suggestions regarding who should be the next doctor from where we can actually get help! One of his friends told us the exact place that can help us. But being into this war, we were aware of the procedures which might be asked by the doctor afterwards. So we didn't want to waste our time and we already gave the blood tests of Aarushi before visiting the doctor suggested by Aakash's friend.

As I didn't rustle up anything to eat, I hurried up and made 'upma' (a South Indian dish) just for Aakash as he had to rush for his office too. Then after packing the food I relinquished the box to him where Aakash briefed me that he will come to the hospital directly from his workplace. After the assemblage of her blood tests reports which will be ready by 1 or 1:30 pm. I agreed and decided to take Aarushi for the checkup. As soon as Aakash left by almost 11 or 11:30 am, the principal of my school Mrs Gardner along with my coordinator Mrs Amita Chaudhary visited at home to see Aarushi as she was her favorite child because of the special attachment ma'am always had with her from the very beginning so they came to see how is she doing!

Ma'am went inside Aarushi's room. I was busy serving her some snacks and juice but she denied and instead she just said 'Shruti I don't feel like eating anything because, eating snacks won't calm me down after checking her health and all I want is to take her to the hospital'. I apprised ma'am that the appointment has been booked already at the hospital as well as there was absenteeism from my husband but she made evident that she doesn't want to wait for anyone. She asked me to call Aakash and inform him that she will be taking Aarushi to the hospital right away as the principal ma'am couldn't comprehend her anymore in the condition of severe illness. On that day my daughter was not at all conscious, she was not eating anything. Even though the juice had to be fed by the spoon, she kept sleeping for hours. I used to try to wake her up for some time but her eyes were not in a condition to be ready to soak up some light or sleepy enough not to be awakened by anyone.

Ma'am tried her best to wake her up by being sedentary next to Aarushi and calling her name again and again. Saying that 'Aarushi! Aarushi! see I am here.' I also said, 'Wake up Aarushi and see Gardner ma'am is here to meet you' but she was not in her senses. She didn't listen to any of our voices. I called my husband to let him know what ma'am has been insisting to do from the time she was in the house as we had an appointment at the hospital. At the same time, how was I supposed to give my denial in front of ma'am? So I was too bewildered in order to take the next step but Aakash asked me not to worry or to be panicked and instead of feeling dilemmas, he just made me feel positive by saying 'There must be something good for our daughter if that's what the situation is standing in front of us. So let's forget about the appointment we made and I will come back to the home where we will take her to the hospital along with ma'am.'

Aakash came home in about 10 minutes and we took our car. Ma'am helped Aarushi sit in the car. We then went to the Synergy hospital Dehradun as ma'am had a few contacts. Me and my husband were discussing the facts with smiles and laughs on our faces in the relaxing tone that 'Everything will be good now; it's good ma'am has come so you know what will happen next? Aarushi will be put on with some fluids for a few hours which will help her to regain her strength as well as her condition will be improved too.'

I was telling Aakash where my clothes are being kept, what all things to get from home, what to eat for dinner and it was comfortable for the travel part as the hospital was quite near from our home. Aakash said it's fine. There's no need to worry about their food because they can eat something from the canteen of the hospital itself and afterwards they will leave for home. So the moment was filled with happiness as well as satisfaction that Aarushi is in good hands now. Ma'am got Aarushi admitted to the emergency ward but the doctor was on rounds and till that time the whole examination process had to start by their end. They started with checking her temperature, blood pressure, etc. Principal ma'am had to leave as it was the time of the final bell, meaning it was time to terminate the day at school and coordinator ma'am also used to go by school bus. Due to the school administrative responsibilities, for them it was kind of hard to stay back at the hospital for any more time but we were assured by ma'am that Aarushi will be fine and the doctor will treat her soon. We took a long breath of comfort and ma'am also left.

CHAPTER FIVE

Ten Minutes Later

11th September 2017

10 minutes later,

The doctor came back after completing his rounds. He examined Aarushi's condition and then called both of us. From there we got the shocking news that her condition is too serious. After listening to this, our brains stopped working and for a few minutes, we stood there like a couple of statues. We couldn't understand what happened to her as it was a piece of unanticipated news. How the cloud of sadness ripped over us! There was no one in the hospital except me and Aakash. Aakash's parents were in the U.S. at that time. So we started to brood about what will happen in the coming moments. I called my mother, standing next to Aarushi and told her that 'Mom I am really not able to understand what is going on here, the doctor made an adage about my daughter's circumstances, just come soon to me please.'

My mother got scared and she came all the way back from Jalandhar with my brother Ritish as well as my aunt to Dehradun. But those 5 to 6 hours where all we did was squander, were the toughest and equally critical. More relatives came by to the hospital to support us.

Aarushi was in the ICU where I was sitting outside in hope to know anything regarding her health. But they wouldn't utter a single word out of their mouths about her condition and I wasn't even allowed to meet her. My mind was getting disconcerted as the time passed by. I didn't know what my daughter was going through inside the ICU, how painful it must be for her! After being impatient, I made a call to my coordinator and I begged her for help because I was too scared with the thoughts in my head. What if the hospital staff won't give her the proper medication at this critical time? Or might experiment with their logic which wouldl make her condition even worse.

MY THOUGHTS WERE DESTROYING ME.

I TRIED NOT TO THINK BUT THE SILENCE WAS A KILLER TOO.

When I called my coordinator, nobody at the hospital was talking to me or telling me anything, at least to calm me so I could rest my petrifying thoughts. I just asked ma'am to elucidate in pellucid words that my daughter has already been through hell as well as tons of experimentation for years. So now they shouldn't even try to apply any kind of experimental treatment over Aarushi.

I needed to know the truth as the nightfall time was approaching and I was being blindsided with some horrible thoughts which were running through my mind, since they broke the shocking news to us. The coordinator ma'am called me back after briefing the hospital faculty as well as the doctor about Aarushi's past struggles in her life in order to inform me; they did respond with 'Everything will be told the way it will be.' Around 6:30 pm the doctor called me after which I called my husband so we both could meet him. We went upstairs in the ICU but who knew that it's going to be a nightmare as another shocking news was about to be announced. The doctor told us that Aarushi has to be shifted to Delhi for her further treatment because **"It's a liver failure"** and she doesn't have much time.

Aakash was shocked to the core as everyone knows about the attachment of a father to his daughter. But since I was the one who would take Aarushi to each and every treatment, I was quite strong at that moment with the hope of betterment. I didn't let any second go to waste and asked the doctor as to how we could save my daughter's life. The doctor told me that the immediate step which we had to take in order to save her was to shift her right away. He took all her medical history. I agreed to start the shifting process but in return, I wanted an ambulance and a doctor from the Synergy hospital in order to restrict any further complications. By the time all the horrifying situation was happening, my brother and mother also reached the hospital too where I let them know about Aarushi's condition and what has to be done next but you know what!

Till the time when I was giving my family a heads up, I actually wasn't aware of the term 'Liver Failure' because still, I remember that I thought it must be some kind of acute damage that was curable. And the family supported me too. My in laws were calming me down. Aarushi was a part of their heart which they loved more than anyone else. I knew it is a big shock for them too. But as they had been so supportive throughout the process so far, similarly they held their nerves and tried to calm me down in the situation and constantly forwarded their support towards me.

I had the belief that whatever misfortune was happening would come to an end soon. I went downstairs where Aakash asked to pack our stuff. He was heading to complete the formalities at the hospital. We had to leave for Delhi but instead of helping us by shifting Aarushi early, the hospital protocol didn't let us leave the place even after we told them that we will be paying every penny of the hospital bill and there was no reason to doubt our intentions. We got free from all the formalities by 9 pm. It was some hospital policy so we had to do everything according to their instructions only. And finally we got the ambulance and a doctor where my brother Ritish stood next to Aarushi in every possible manner. He told her that 'See Aarushi Mamu is here' and after so long she opened her eyes a bit just after listening to my brother's voice as she was very attached to him.

Every person from our family was standing in front of me while we took Aarushi inside of the ambulance to shift her to Delhi and at the same time Aakash also stepped one step ahead, came closer to me, and said 'Shruti, do you understand she had liver failure?' And I replied to him with ease as well as confidence in my tone that 'Yes! No issues, it would be fine'. Which was not at all true because I did not know enough to answer in the way I did. Aakash again tried to explain to me that we had to arrange a new liver for her. We would need a lot of money in order to organize it soon. But again I replied in a boisterous tone not to worry as everything will be done and if we had to sell ourselves then we would do that too.

A donor's liver to save her life had a cost of 25 to 30 lakhs but where would we arrange for the money! And at that very moment, I wasn't caring about the expenses because all I could think about was my daughter, who was not just suffering but battling for her life. No one ate anything since morning because our appetite was dead. We reached Delhi early in the morning by 3 am. The doctors admitted Aarushi in an emergency department where her body was too stiff to take out her night wear which she hadn't changed since home. They had to cut out her clothes and it was a moment filled with pain, the pain which is still contemporary and hits us like it happened yesterday.

The doctor provided us the same information we had before which was 'She is too critical' and they had to run different tests on her. She has been kept in the ICU where we again started completing the formalities. They asked us to wait outside so me and my husband were sitting in the waiting lounge, by 6 am doctors called us to take her medical history as well as ask for her details, and the moment we were about to leave the ICU; an insane voice started hitting my ears which was Aarushi's and she was calling me Mumma! Mumma!

Aakash told me that it was not possible as she was sedated so how could she speak? But I told him that believe me, Aarushi is calling me and my husband kept telling me that I might be hallucinating. While we were having the conversation, a nurse came after looking for me and took me inside the ICU. I went inside where I saw her and she was sedated, she was not conscious but still she was screaming her lungs out by calling Mumma! Mumma! I was asked by the doctors to calm her as they explained to me about the complications of her shouting which would have affected her brain. I had to calm her down in order to save her from further dreadful complications. I couldn't deliberate anything better to make a stronger connection with her so I started reciting a poem which I used to sing when she was a small kid and I have been told that she could still hear me even her consciousness was zero and how could I forget about the poems she has written for me, all were running through my mind at the same time.

MOM

Maybe, I don't thank you at all times,
Maybe, my love for you is lacking behind,
But not to worry it's just 2018
We have to walk together, a thousand miles.

Aashii! That 5 letters name you gave,
Yes! It's my fav
It was so satisfactory
When you exclaimed

"Ma'am a test to be done"
Now, this was usual to me,
But still, I said "No, don't do that"
Said you... "don't worry, sit on my lap"

Scopy's and MRIs were my big enemies,
But I had to go through by any means,
"Hold my hands tight, Aashii you have to fight"
You are a source of satisfaction; you made
I believe that everything will be alright.

Ah! Sorry for the heartbreak I gave you a few months ago!
It's a big amount that I owe,
Thank you for saving me from this quake,
I saw you standing beside me, all awake.

If at times I seemed ungrateful,
I apologize for that mommy
Nothing you have done can be forgotten
And day by day, you mean more to me!

-Aarushi Prabhakar
13/03/18

And this is how she used to express herself, not just thoughts but the way of loving too which always made me feel special as well as closer to her in every possible aspect. She was experiencing a kind of blessing as her life started breathing altogether, without any life supporters. She couldn't forget about how it happened! Even though she had big enemies to deal with, there she was! Filled with hope and courage where it looked like I wasn't just dictating her to fight but it was an affirmation for my soul too.

CHAPTER SIX

The Childhood Times

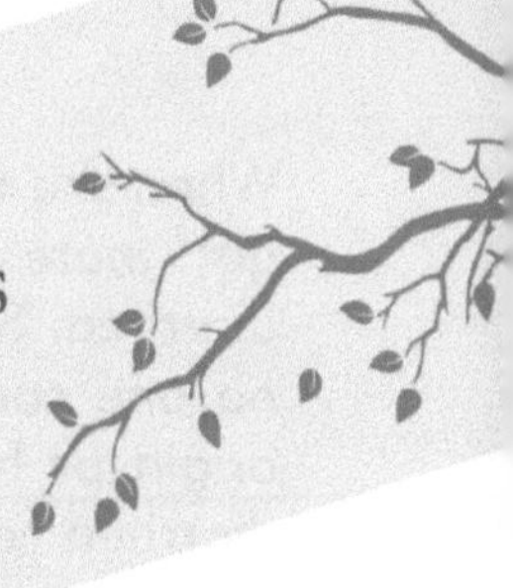

As we all know how salient childhood is for all of us and distinctively when we grow, in the same way it was a prime center of attention for Aarushi too but again, there was no time she did live without so much struggle. From her birth till 3 to 4 years of her life, she was normal just like other kids; there were no signs of being bilious at the peak level or even reaching that stage. When she was stepping into her 5th year of her life, she did develop a problem of constipation as well as diarrhea, which was happening repeatedly. It was not getting a rest due to which our terms got changed from the 'problem' to 'disease'.

At the initial stage of her birth, she was coming unstruck to constipation. But we took the problem in a casual form like other newborns certainly face it too, otherwise there was no other problem which can refer to genetic or happened due to any kind of medication.

When she turned 6 years old, the episodes of the motion got more frequent and she started struggling with diarrhea. She had been taken to many local doctors but no one could tell us what the problem was, what's the origin or how it could be cured. Also, we always take diarrhea or constipation as 'not such a big deal' statement, it just got worse with the time where no medication was working for her, the treatment started all over again in Delhi which involved many hospitals like the Institute of Liver and Biliary Sciences, Max, AIIMS, Medanta as well as Ganga Ram. The local doctors of Dehradun couldn't help us with the answers but at last, Aarushi's condition got settled with Dr. Pankaj Vohra who is gastrointestinal specialist, was placed in Max Hospital only, where he used to do his private practice in the Khan market.

He started providing her with a little dose of steroids and almost every hospital doctor asked for an endoscopy test. In the end, she finally got suspected with different diseases like Crohn's colitis, Inflammatory Bowel Disease (IBD) or irritable bowel syndrome (IBS). But my point stands still till the present date that I don't think it was true at all because it was something doctors suspected and not proven! Not even a single endoscopy result has shown a sign of any chronic illness as whenever her intestines were in the shadow tests, there was nothing; which means if anyone still asks me whether she suffered from these diseases? I would reply no! Not in my knowledge. But again just because of her loose stools, these diseases were in the line of conjecture.

She also got treated by Dr. Seema Alam and they tried different treatment regimens by stopping the consumption of wheat, as they gave their thought towards some allergic reaction but her condition was consistent and there wasn't any improvement. Another time, she prescribed to rustle up her meals only in coconut oil, to cease dairy products as well as vitamin C. We all were really bothered about the intake of it because the moment she used to eat anything which contained vitamin C she always had diarrhea but even after all of the effort this idea also fell in the hole of darkness.

And guess what? Starting from around 2006 till 2013, Aarushi faced intolerance of many things which came in the list to keep a child healthy but for her, it was not less than any poisoning product. Every year in the repetition of 2 to 3 times, she had to go for her endoscopy, routine check-up.

And after reading the details till now, I think you all must be getting to know that my daughter was just under the experimentation for years where no doctor had anything to tell us with the surety about what the diagnosis was? Or what my little girl was going through! It is really getting hard for me to express all over again while writing the story as it becomes fresh like 'the pain never ended' which I don't feel will ever come to an end!

Aarushi was on steroids from 2007 to 2013 where initially the doctor started with the light dose but there were times when her condition would fall, her dose of steroids would be increased and when she used to stabilize, the dose was reduced. This process kept going on without a pause. Whenever we used to take her to Dr.Vohra, all we did discuss how many mg of steroid should be provided to Aarushi for her present condition but then who would like keeping themselves on medicines over years, there will be a day when the anger, frustration, a phase of exertion and you will be worn out of the situation no matter how ill you are!

And this is exactly what has happened with Aarushi too, she stopped taking every medicine which was a part of her daily life routine, treatments involving her endoscopy, or visiting doctors anymore in the year 2013 as she was exasperated with living with support instead of living on her own.

I understood her pain because it's impossible to surround a 3-time meal filled with medicines. She had lost her joy of enjoying the different tastes of food where she made her denial too clear as well as loud enough that she won't be going into the phase she did spend 7 to 8 years of her life.

We didn't stop! Of course, being a mother, all I wanted was to find a cure for her because I wanted to see my daughter live every bit of her life without being scared of who knows what might happen next! I always used to stand in front of her and tell her about the enemies she had to face, 'the tests'. But there is a saying, 'You can't feel the same pain or understand anyone else's situation or the condition they have been suffering till you tip your toes in their shoes'. My daughter stopped thinking about her illness not because she had lost her hope to become healthy but all she wanted was just to live and to take her life not towards the path of right regimen but towards being normal like any other kid would be at her age.

Today, I am able to understand her, about how badly she had the aspiration towards things to stay just in the ordinary format without any routine check-up, but when she was with all of us we could think of how to fasten her health in order to make her dream possible. We always had a hope that one day, we would keep moving forward to achieve happiness.

The next destination was Ayurvedic medication. When we went back to Jalandhar, we had been dispensed with an aspiration that the condition of the ailment she kept tormenting can be cured through Ayurveda. So, we consulted an ayurvedic doctor too and there were no problems with the intake of new medicines but there was the absence of the virtuoso improvement for which we hoped we would see. My family also placed their pronouncement about her intake of medicines or steroids.!

They objected to the excessive usage of many medicines and the procedures she went through. She hadn't been doing good, but under doctors' experiment as well as her intoxicated body with the chemicals and eventually, nothing worked so my family asked us to give her some treatment which won't harm her any further. If nothing can be effective, at least there would be no harm to her and for the next 3 to 4 years. She was doing well, we hoped for the bright light behind the darkness again.

CHAPTER SEVEN

The Longest Hope

The requirement of the transplant got out of our hands because we didn't think about what would be the next possibility, we were just walking on a road with no lights where we had no idea about where we were heading! Dr. Subhash Gupta notified us in a diaphanous way as well as an upfront statement that she needs an emergency liver transplant which can't wait for the long list of prioritizing the damage as her brain got affected with the complication of an infection mentioned before. If we waited or did nothing for the next 24 hours, we wouldn't be able to save her life. While I was in the market for the preparations of documentation needed in the procedure of liver transplant to make sure that every given criterion should get approved, my husband was going under some diagnostic tests to see if he would be able to qualify in order to become the donor for Aarushi but there was nothing that has happened with ease. So how is it that this time it would have taken place with no problems. The moment test results came, it showed that Aakash doesn't fit into the category in order to provide his liver to Aarushi because his liver was 'fatty' which is not healthy for the transplant.

After this complication, I also went through the same diagnostic tests but already plenty of salient time was progressing rapidly. Aakash's tests itself ended by evening and then mine got concluded by 12 or 1 am. At least we all were relieved with the results that my liver was perfectly healthy and I was fit for the donation. On the other side, she kept screaming, "Mumma! Mumma!" while she was in the ICU and the doctor had to keep her sedated afterward to resolve her so that she doesn't put a strain on herself, especially before the surgery.

Everyone was too tense with the situation as well as worried about the outcomes. I should mention even for the present time that no one knew what would happen in the very next moment. On the same day, committee also stepped in to check up on the relations as well as to complete every single legal work that has to be done by the government where they also called my brother in order to take all the confirmation that "Is there any chance we were going under the donation process under pressure or anything against our own will?" Even though I was the donor, they prepared me with the real fact that if I do not come out of the operation room alive, what would be my last wish? If I had to convey any message or meet someone before going inside the operation room.

In the end, I was declared to be the perfect person for the donation. By 1:30 am, we were allotted a room at the hospital. I never knew that it would be something which did not take place in an acute form, I was strong enough to pull my daughter out of hell. But somewhere my heartbeats used to race whenever I thought that her liver was not partially damaged but we were informed that there must be only 5% left of her liver on which she was alive but still, I knew my daughter was a combatant and nothing will ensue in her life. Everyone was worn out enough that they would pass the moment they lay themselves over the bed; as in the past 2 days and nights not just me but my husband and brother didn't even take a nap. I was the donor so I had to stay where I was accompanied with my brother as well as my husband and Aarushi was under observation in the ICU. I can't demonstrate the time we were going through, our bodies and minds were exhausted in a way that we couldn't even sleep for some time. After 30-45 minutes, the nurses came in to draw me up for the surgery which was the first thing proceeding to happen in the morning and afterwards, the nurse told us to rest ourselves for a few hours then I shall be shifted to the OT by 7 am.

On 13th September 2017, I went to the operation theater by 7 am, where every person in my family was perturbed for me. My husband started distressing himself that both core parts of his heart will be battling from death but again, I told them that I was brawny enough to skirmish and not just me but Aarushi will also come back with the positive news. It might be hard to trust my coming statement but 'I didn't cry, my tears just did not fall off my eyes because I had to stay filled with all the courage in my veins and I knew I couldn't fall as I had to rescue my daughter'. Inside the OT when I was being shifted over the operation table, they asked me about my last wish too!

I answered that 'I just want to see my daughter once' and the doctors told me that it can't happen as they will be transferring my daughter to the room I was residing after which they sedated me as she was already on the life-supporting machine hence, I agreed with their views.

The surgery finished by 6 pm which means the operation kept going on for 10 to 11 hours and our ears finally received some good news that 'It was a successful surgery'. While in between the operation if any doctor came out of the operation theater, my brother and husband would extract any information about what was taking place or whether everything was fine?

They both were taking care of everything. In that moment of time, Ritish was more responsible than any of us because on the day of surgery my husband was all numbed as well as quite in sadness.

The pain after surgery was anonymous and it couldn't be ever expressed in words as I also had some issues related to UTI (urinary tract infection). By the evening, while I was recovering from the anesthesia, everyone approached to meet me while Aarushi was transferred in the liver ICU. We all were relieved that now artifacts will be fine but later, we were being informed that the starting two days are treacherous as well as censorious for the recipient and nothing yet can be proclaimed regarding her health until the time she will be awake.

However, Dr. Gupta would work according to his gut feeling, he notified them with ease that she would be fine. The 3rd day I got to know via the nurse who was monitoring her and no one was allowed to meet her in the liver ICU. Instead of observing her on the screen, Aarushi did wake up once and asked for the ice cream, no one could ever chronicle the feeling I was experiencing beneath my skin. It was such a split second of relaxation that she was reverberating just like herself but then with time she started recuperating, though no one was still authorized to meet her, she started talking on a call with her father and I was at peace that finally she will subsistence with no problems.

One thing which Aarushi didn't know was what had happened to her because the last time she was in her conscious state, she got admitted to Synergy hospital. She was clueless about the liver failure or anything related to the transplant but a nurse filled her in with all the information about what her condition was or why she came to Max hospital.

So, it was an evident part where Aarushi interrogated about who donated the liver to her. The nurse told her that

'Your mother donated her liver to you' and guess what! She started getting some dreadful thoughts like "My mother donated her liver to me and I am exceptionally fine but what about her condition, whether she is in comfort or not?" In short, she was terrified with the thought, what if she lives and I die!

Aarushi started screaming in stubbornness to see whether I was all right or not! I was in such pain that I couldn't handle my tears this time as she did not believe the nurse's statement at all. Who knows if the nurse would recline too! And if she pronounced something, no one could stop her from doing what she desires. So, I went inside her room with the help of a wheelchair, just to show her that I was doing good, alive and nobody was reclining. We both saw each other and there were just tears in silence and we both said nothing for a few minutes, the cheerfulness was overloaded when I went to sit next to my daughter. We had a conversation for almost 30 minutes as I explained to her about the condition that there will be no problems stirring us anymore because 'the liver is an organ which will grow eventually with a good blood supply and her previous conditions regarding her health will be concluded completely'. I had to leave my room as well because the pain was becoming unbearable and it was just increasing by sitting longer on a wheelchair. So, she took a promise from me that I will visit her two times a day; morning and evening. How could I not tell you all, patiently reading every aspect of what she has to say.

WHAT ELSE SHALL I WISH FOR?

What else shall I wish for?
When I have got the best
Who is so supportive and loving?
Who is different from the rest?

What else shall I wish for?
When she gives me what I need?
The one who is understanding,
The one who is so sweet.

What else shall I wish for?
When I have her, who is so outstanding,
When I have got the one who gave me wings
The one whom I love beyond everything!

Aarushi Prabhakar
10/05/2019
[Mother's Day poem for mamma]

After 5 days, I got transferred to a normal room while Aarushi was still in the liver ICU but as I have already mentioned that how obstinate she was, she did the same part all over again, Aarushi also wanted to be shifted to my room itself along with me but there was another patient. We notified her about the discussions we were having with the doctor that if her health is fine enough to be shifted from the ICU then they would transfer her to my room. It was a night of laughter where my husband and my brother Ritish didn't sleep, they were awake until morning. We were cackling with joy and contentment because we had this opportunity after so long that we couldn't remember when we had a room filled with laughter. I had to ask them to stop making me laugh as my stitches started prickling. On the 6th day just after 24 hours, Aarushi also got transferred into my room with a beautiful south Indian look, braided hair, little black bindi over her forehead, eyeliner; she was looking too cute, and then we had a family dinner together by 10 pm. It felt like a moment of never-ending joyfulness which I wanted to freeze forever. We stayed for 18 to 20 days in the hospital after which she was doing better, her condition as well as the recovery rate was faster than mine and seeing that, I was happiest on the earth.

Later on, she headed with many restrictions regarding her diet, medicines, and what not was added to the list but I didn't hesitate this time because I knew it would do only better now. She had to wait to eat her restricted diet food 1 hour prior to taking her medication, which involved steroids. After a month we stayed in Ghaziabad for a few days because I was facing an issue with UTI which increased after the operation. My daughter was fine so we went back to Dehradun, our home after my health recovered where I couldn't trust over time that the cloud of darkness did shred away and we did make it which no one else could have thought that we would be able to enlighten her life again.

The journey of 2017 to 2018 was blissful for her, she was fully recovering from her health condition which held upon her for years and there you go.

OCEAN'S TALK

Lying on the sand,
The wind whispered in my ear,
it was not really planned,
What I went through the year.

Mind was in a constant run
Wondering if a riptide sea,
A pirate on the ship,
Now buried really deep.

I liked the sharp salty smell there,
The vastness of the blue
The secrets that I shared,
It was easier to bid adieu!

Ocean gave me strength,
A life to hire,
Emotions were intense

That evening was really sensitive
Aarushi Prabhakar
11/04/2018

In April, she wrote about something from where she came back after walking down the dangerous battle of life or death. Aarushi was getting her strength back, her hopes were high that now she will be going to live her life in rest where no one would be in a rush.

CHAPTER EIGHT

Just Great Times!

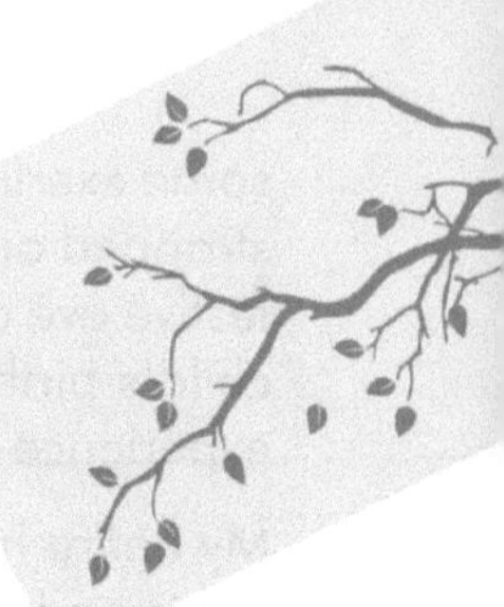

In September 2017,

Aarushi got her liver transplant done. She rested for about 2 months, as you must be knowing that after transplant a patient has to be careful regarding many things as she was on immunosuppressants, she was not allowed to evacuate anywhere and there were certain restrictions on food.

Only me and my husband were allowed to have a seat in her room at home; we needed to save her from any kind of infection which could have been dangerously effective to her health. She was supposed to wear a mask while she had to move around but these all things were exasperating for Aarushi, as she was not a girl of a gene who could sit hushed in one room. She was full of life and wanted to live her life all-inclusively. She wanted to have her friends gathered around, her relatives or anyone close to surround her with. I waited dispassionately to describe an episode concerning her.

In the year 2017, Diwali was on 18th October (Wednesday) which was her treasured festival. Every year she was the one who gave hand in the department of spangling the entire house with beautiful yellow flowers and the Rangoli was always the center of her consciousness as well as an exciting part to do. Just imagine she had her major surgery a month ago, her strength was hardly manufactured in her to participate in some exertion but I have no idea how she managed to be strapped around the clock, we were all very excited for the festive eve as it was real life-celebration of Diwali after the child's birth. The feeling was not any subsidiary than the experience of exultation when my princess got a new life.

My entire house had been lit with beautiful candles, fairy lights and we put 108 diyas too. While I was busy lighting the diyas, Aarushi came to me and said, 'Do you know that we all are able to celebrate Diwali only because of me! As if something would have happened to me then you all couldn't celebrate and would have been sitting quietly till now.'

I was really unmindful of the fact that I just have 2 more years to celebrate with her. Days went by like this. We were taking special care of our princess. As it was wintertime, we kept her inside that year. Her birthday, which is on 30th December, was also celebrated with great joy. Aakash booked a hotel for her birthday party where some of her friends were invited and a gala dinner was served. Aarushi was too happy that day. She really looked like Cinderella in that beautiful peach gown with her heels on. That birthday was an exceptionally foremost day in its own way and then we welcomed the new year.

Everything was going well where she insisted on annexing the school. I took the authorization from her doctor, though she was allowed to go to school, she had to follow the rules strictly made to keep up with her health like her table had to be sanitized congruously. There were certain restrictions like she was not allowed to attain a seat with a child who had a cold or fever, couldn't share her lunch box and the most salient topic was that when she was on steroids so she used to perceive hunger after every half an hour. Therefore, I had to pack 2 to 3 lunch boxes for her, she used to be selective regarding her food as well and because of her scrupulous behavior, I had to be vigilant but I must say, Aarushi always said that her school is her secondary home.

When she started visiting her school all over back in January then my mind used to get worried as well as disconcerted at the same time but she used to say, "Mumma! The moment I step inside the school, I discern recovered" and that statement of hers was honest as her actions matched her phrase. Aarushi appeared for her concluding examination of 11th standard and she got 3rd position in her class. It was a great acquisition, all the teachers, principal ma'am were content with her staging.

In April, she got placed in class 12th, she always had her eyes towards the head girl title of her school. But there is a famous saying, 'Man proposes and God disposes of', Aarushi also desired to take her

school to new heights, there was not a single activity where she didn't participate. Debating was her favorite field where she represented herself at inter-school competitions. At last, in the month of May, Aarushi was proclaimed to be the consummate student of her house (Gardener House).

She was feeling joyful on that day, we as parents were invited to the investiture ceremony at her school where her grandfather also accompanied us. We were also called on the stage to put on her badge. It was a proud moment for us when her name was announced by Ma'am Michelle (vice-principal) inaugurating the candidates to the audience and as I apprehend about an announcement of her, the audience was applauding for her achievements which were loud enough to announce her as an extraordinary child accumulating an extraordinary talent. There were tears of joy in my eyes which was apparent for a proud mother and that day, I had a feeling of getting successful with a satisfactory percentage.

Aarushi looked really smart as well as confident in her uniform which was also pinned with the prefect badges on the straps over her shoulders. Till that time things were going well with her health; she was enjoying every moment of her life which was getting ordinary exactly the way she wanted and it gave us a long breath of moderation.

CHAPTER NINE

Farewell Of Life

Aarushi was such a girl who would never back down even though her health had become the biggest issue in between the happiness of living her best ordinary life. On September 5th, 2018 she and many students of her batch had contributed their time to put on an amazing show for teachers' day. Aarushi was managing all her responsibilities even with her ascites, she was leading her house sincerely. She made the day special for teachers as well as along with her co-prefects she was in charge of. All the preparations where the choreography of the dance performance was done by Aarushi herself, the gifts were pleasing which had to be given to the principal ma'am, coordinators and also for other teachers.

The whole initiative was looking at its best as my daughter really has done her work the way she does it, there were games for the teachers, and also few were given contrasting tags and sashes like Miss diligent, Miss beautiful, etc. A special gift was given to the teachers by her which was a hoarding of flex where she made the school tree describing the role and significance of every single teacher.

If we talk about her health then it was really in a bad condition on that day as her ascites have increased where she was over-embellished managing the teacher's day program, I have no idea how she bore the anonymous amount of pain. Due to her ascites, she generated a phobia of stepping over the stairs. She had enlightened her friends that they should clasp her while she would be taking her steps but the co-host forgot to hold her. She fell on the stairs from the frontal region where her bloated stomach got badly hurt and there was a loud noise in the auditorium as it was full of children as well as teachers.

Action had been taken immediately as Aarushi's friend took her in his arms and went directly to the infirmary where the principal ma'am, Michelle ma'am was there with her and I was informed too. The moment I entered the infirmary, I saw my daughter smiling, telling me that she is just fine and no one has to agonize but in the meantime, I called Aakash and subsequently planned to take her to Delhi for her problem. Later with the time, Ma'am Michelle said that the show won't continue but Aarushi insisted not to stop the program as everyone along with her worked really hard in order to organize the special occasion.

On her request, ma'am went back to the auditorium and there was a surprise that happened. Aarushi joined back after 10 minutes to host the further program. Ma'am asked her to sit on the chair as well. The sweetest and thoughtful part was when my daughter was asked to keep sitting while hosting the show. I had to say that because of ma'am I acquired three bonus years to reside with my child and I don't have any words to thank her enough for pushing us not to make any delay for Aarushi's checkup in 2017. On 6th September, we took her to Delhi and the discovered part will be revealed later.

In 2018, Aarushi was back to school after some time where she was preparing for her 12th board examination. The health issues were constant but again she was doing well, it always looked like that she had an extraordinary gift and I was inspired to watch her living big without cribbing over situations.

Now an exciting day has come for which every student has awaited for a long time. It was the 'farewell time' for class 12th students. In our school, the farewell used to happen on a large scale like some fancy party accumulating beautiful decorations, the auditorium seemed like some fairyland where the dress codes were also decided. The girls had to wear saree and boys had to be dressed up in a suit to give a gentleman look. Later, I and Aarushi went shopping for her farewell dress where my daughter's choice was different from others; she told me not to obtain anything which accommodates shiny material or even a little bit of shimmer over the saree.

We ordered a bottle green color saree but there was an issue regarding her appearance as she was too thin as well as her body weight was not like any other kid of her age. So, my husband thought of making her wear a salwar suit in order to comfort her rather than putting her into discomfort or in any challenging situation. But, as usual, she loved challenges. She decided to wear the saree itself; also, we selected a beautiful blouse of bottle green color with some embroidery on. The next stop was to select the jewelry piece and I had to say that her choice was elegant as she chose long earrings with beads and emeralds as well as a bracelet full of studs. The footwear was also the fancy one as she bought 'heels' golden in colour.

The parlor appointment was booked but she denied to take the services as she wanted to look the way she looked in her real-life without any extra additional beauty-enhancing procedures. All the work was done for her farewell preparations but suddenly, a thought clicked in my mind about the cold weather as it was the month of December. So, it was an unfeasible fact that if she had to manage without her woolens, to make her look gorgeous at the same time excluding the woolens what else could I have done! Not just her wish was to go different but I played a part too by making her wear a velvet long blouse of maroon in color instead of a casual one and the new blouse was made overnight as the next morning was Aarushi's farewell.

I woke her up as she had an appointment at the parlor just for her dressing and a bit of touchup. We outstretched school at a given time which was 11 am sharp and every teacher commended her beautiful look which was actually pretty as well as elegant at the same time, exactly the way Aarushi wanted. The ramp walk round started and the opening had been done by none other but my beautiful daughter, the confidence while walking through the round in good inches was marvelous and after making it through the top 15, she stepped in the last round accumulating 6 other girls where every single person had to answer the questions asked by the judges. She has been asked, 'Where do you see yourself in 20 years?'

The question was interesting but her answer made the question even worth asking her. She said that 'I see myself in a very nice place with a wonderful job where I could make my family and my school proud of me. I just want to earn that much with which I am able to keep my family happy and healthy.' And guess what! After this answer of her, the princess of St. Judes was decided which was undoubtedly my daughter, who won the title.

My happiness and excitement knew no boundaries after the announcement as she really looked like a princess the moment she wore that beautiful crown. It was not the end of surprises as she also won the title of 'THE PRIDE' of our school. The day was beautiful, especially the time when her small clip played on the screen of the auditorium with the song 'Dil hai Chota sa Choti si Asha'. The video showed the whole journey starting from the first day till last and I was thrilled with the gesture shown to my daughter. It must be special for her but being a mother when you get to see your child getting praised with the utmost gestures then your head is always held higher and higher by adding some of the happiness as well as proud feeling.

Everyone was happy for her achievements and as her final board examination was approaching, she pushed herself in the preparations but her health wasn't allowing the strength. She badly needed to keep up with her studies and one week before her examinations, she got hold of Jaundice all over again. I tried my best in convincing her to drop the year as her health was deteriorating but she didn't stop and she just uttered a line which said, 'Mother, I will manage'. My mind stops working after thinking about how much she manages? How much did she give herself to participate in being ordinary? The results came and it was unbelievable because it showed that she literally managed! She passed with 89% marks on the 12th board.

She was always praised for her will power which was more than any of us present at home right now and maybe that's what she always tried to teach me too. Even in her absence and as she was a bright child, there were many teachers who knew her not just in a way of a student but also as a person where many messages have been bombarded from her schoolmates and teachers as well.

A little girl passed through the gate of St. Jude's and lit up everyone around her. Once I saw her, sitting in the sun and I went to speak to her. With a smile on her face, she said her name was Aarushi Prabhakar. This is how we were introduced. Later on, over the years Aarushi's name was everywhere, whether it was debate or drama. This little girl took part in all the activities with a lot of grace and I saw her grow from a little girl to a confident young teenager. School activities gave her the strength to overcome all that she was going through in her life and at school, we often remember her and talk about her talents. She fought the odds with courage and I will always remember her as the brave, humble little girl who always had a smile on her face.

By Amita Chaudhary

Knowing Aarushi was one of the best things that happened to me. There were times when we didn't talk at all. She, being my senior, had responsibilities to fulfill, she was the house captain and had tons of school responsibilities plus her being a perfect student, she was involved in extracurricular activities as well. I remember whenever there used to be an inter-house dance competition, she used to lead the pack, she was every teacher's favorite student where you can sense how good she was. We could talk about anything to her, she was completely chill with everything and always had a positive aura. I used to bore her whenever we met because she always used to be a listener, always being there for people whenever they needed someone, especially a person to talk to. I could trust her with everything and anything doesn't matter if it's my work life or personal, she never judged me for my wrong choices. Somehow, I knew she wouldn't judge me. That's why I went up to her in the first place whenever there used to be a mishap.

Aarushi knew very well that I can't study, especially when there was history and physics. Well, she couldn't help me with physics as she had commerce, but she did help me with history by giving her notes and everything she could help with. I couldn't have graduated from 11th grade if she hadn't been on my nerves. I know what I was like before I met her and how much I have learned from her,

I wouldn't be what I am today if it wasn't for her, if today I am a good person, she does have her hands in that.

By- Yuvraj (Aarushi's friend)

The waves of time rushed up the shores of memory, receding to reveal the pearls of action of the bravest embedded in the sands of time. Their brilliance dazzles us, awe-inspiring- such a gem was Aarushi. She walked into my class, a tiny smile on her lips which implied serious fun. She was par excellence, life with a theme. She was quite the best rolled into one. Prolific writer, a brilliant debater and artist, a dancer, a vibrant YouTuber, an excellent planner, and more importantly an excellent human being. Unfortunately, illness is indiscriminate in its choice of victim, choosing regardless of age and goodness.

Life suddenly took a u-turn and became all about hospitals, IVs, medication routines. Instead of being in the company of her classmates, skipping on a playground, Aarushi found herself in the company of health care workers. This is when her never say die attitude shone the brightest. This girl was resilient and brave in the face of prices that would have made a forty-year-old son shiver. Despite hoping for the best, her liver couldn't keep up. She went for a transplant, her mom (Shruti, the donor). After the surgery, things started taking a turn- she was doing better, it seemed like she had overcome the storm.

She came to visit me and I couldn't help but ask her, "Aarushi, is life worth living?" and this punny girl went ahead and said, "well, it depends on the liver." Little did I know, this was the last time. It did see her, she left as a star, for the stars where celebrities don't go. She lived more in her short life than even 80 years old to impart the lesson that a long life may not be good enough but a good life is indeed long enough. I have learned more here than any other student- her courage and grit were exemplary.

We miss you Aarushi.

Benita Srivastava

Your life was a blessing

Your memory is a treasure

You are loved beyond words

And missed beyond measure

"Don't let what you cannot do interfere with what you can do" yet she wanted to learn anything and everything. She believed in **"the beautiful thing about learning is that no one can take it away from you".** She was a voracious reader. She used to say "Learning is my only motto in life". It is the sole possession that I will be able to augment throughout my life", who knew it was too short for her.

-Mrs. J. Aggarwal

When life got difficult in the middle of a painful hospital procedure Aarushi wrote poetry, made handmade cards, jotted down points for the magazine, went online shopping for her mother, made her father's birthday special. She never stopped caring and with her last ounce of strength, she gave to all those around her.

When a star that shone so bright goes away, the world may seem darker, however please hold on to every memory and message of Aarushi and always know Aarushi is only a thought away.

-Ma'am Michelle.

CHAPTER TEN

A New Chapter

But again, in July she had a problem with ascites (swelling in the abdominal region caused by the accumulation of fluid). We consulted the doctor in Delhi, where we were informed that it happens sometimes as her albumin level has gone down which can be cured by providing her with a protein diet. But being a vegetarian, the easiest part also got converted into tough work. It was impossible to make Aarushi eat eggs or chicken so we had to lie to her about the food she used to take during her meal but it didn't work in any manner.

Later with the diagnosis when the ascites was not settling down, doctors discovered on 6th September 2018 that she had started facing another problem that wasn't supposed to happen but it did happen anyway, this time it was PVT (portal vein thrombosis). There was a partial clot in her portal vein due to which her new liver couldn't get the full supply of blood and again it would damage the liver or I should say many other complications were also frightening. On 13th September 2018, it was her first liver birthday which we celebrated in the hospital itself and we did bring a big cake of liver shape where Dr. Gupta participated in the celebration too.

Now a new treatment regimen was on the list and new disease to battle but my daughter was of such a brave personality that I don't think many people would be, I am not even including myself in the numbers because I was strong for the hope of her betterment but she was someone who would never give up no matter what will happen in the future! The PVT gave her some additional pain which led to the accumulation of fluid in her abdomen and it was getting resolved with medication but sometimes doctors punctured her stomach to drain the fluid.

My hope was not going to end but this time it was hard not because we were just out of the big trauma, but the disease was growing over her where in the beginning the clot was partial in her portal veins and instead of getting cured via whatever doctors could do to help her with the painful symptoms of PVT, the clot was dangerously blocking her whole vein. From 2018 to 2020 it was all about her thrombosis which looked like a never-ending disease and as time was passing, we had a new challenge coming in our way.

To cure the thrombosis, first, they moved forward with the dilation of her portal vein via endoscopy, and the process repeated for 3 to 4 times where the last dilation was considered to be successful as many branches led to liver opened up but still, there was the specific region which couldn't get clot free. The stent was also performed 2 times which functions to maintain the flow of blood but it didn't work either. I did notice with the time that it was the month of September when she always went through the biggest tests of her life.

I started feeling awful about this month because every year in September, doctors claimed that she would need a re-transplant of her liver and it made me feel like it was written to happen that how could she be so badly in this month? It was always filled with frightening as well as bad news.

Whenever Aarushi was in the hospital after her transplantation, we never let the doctor place any conversation in front of her and when we had the talk with the doctor outside of her room. He always mentioned that mostly in PVT cases the liver transplant had to happen where he suggested Aakash maintain his health in order to become the donor. In the initial stage of her problem, the doctors prescribed the medication process as well but if it wouldn't work then rather than accepting the re-transplant there was no other option left for my daughter. What was happening at the moment was the treatment used to make the progress in her health which didn't let re-transplant happen but the cure used to show its effect temporarily.

The re- transplant was risky enough and the chances for the survival chances were too low, it had become a pattern in a way that every time her condition with PVT used to get stabilized, she had the problems related to it as her body did respond to the medication but still it wasn't getting any better for her either, it is insane to quote but after the short-term medication the disease has grown inside her, instead of showing any signs of improvement and I am quoting this statement because this is exactly I did witness. I would like to make it very clear that personally, I won't put blame over anyone because the fact is, it won't work anyway as she will never be coming back to me!

The problem was the failure, not the medication! We were horrified with the part that nothing was curing her in a permanent way; it was always about the fake hope which we had been giving to her that 'Aarushi, just one more procedure and you will be fully cured'. It makes me feel sick that instead of spending any more good time with her, I just provided her with the hollow hope but she was yet ready as a fighter like she has always been.

LIFE I WISHED FOR

Lying on the sand,
The wind whispered in my ears,
It was not really planned,
What I went through years!

My mind was in a constant run,
Wondering on the riptide sea,
The pirate on the ship
Now buried really deep.

My life was not easy to live,
Not like any other child
But I lived it with a smile,
A strong heart and mind.

Doctors-Doctors all around,
I hated medicines
I hated tests

I wished for a life like the rest

I wanted me and my soul to sit together,
To write our destination
So that at the end of this play of life,
I have no complaints, but full satisfaction.

I wish for a life spent well,
So that I have thoughts to dwell on,
I have many memories to carry me away
I lived the life I wished for; I would say!

[This poem is a collaboration of my two poems]

Aarushi Prabhakar

10/01/2018

Tons of heparin injections were injected into her veins, just imagine a person taking 2 injections every day scheduled in the mornings and evenings. And during every CT scan, my brother Ritish used to go with her as well as hold her hands where he kept dictating the steps which were happening with her just to make her feel that she was not alone and the pain will be over soon. Then in 2019, we took her to a new place which was DMC to check again if she can be fully cured of the consistent problems where liver was totally fine, there was no increase or decrease in liver enzymes but loose stools weren't fixed yet. We lived in hope that once the liver transplant will start working properly then her previous problems will get fixed too but whatever we hoped for was never completed in an easy way.

The time we all were battling with her, she didn't stop! No doubt she was strong but the point is; she was also a human being who had a lot to express, a lot to say and I am so proud of her that instead of having all the problems my daughter was someone who never knew the phrase "I can't". I always share her thoughts which should come out loud in front of everyone reading not just my feelings but my daughter too. **An insanely exceptional thought for new life!**

A LIFE IN LINES

A new life has been secured
New competition in this fighting world
A new body to earn, this materialistic trust
Many times, forgets "we are born of it and
we shall return to dust"

Let's start his journey
The lines will tell you where we finish
The end shall be worthy
And the feeling will re-furnish.

Initially, he is the happiest one alive
With each trotting step, he takes
It's the time when he is too innocent,
It's the time which is superb and excellent.

A sudden ban on his head
When he is introduced to books
Welcome to the world of competition
It was the first time he was shaking!

But now when he watches his school bus go by
He knows deep down he wants to cry
The school taught what passion and confidence is
The best part of his life is what he still misses.

College days were more of laughter and fun
Fights, love, quarrel- a life with mixed emotions
Success, failure, joy, and sorrow
It taught him now to work for a better tomorrow.
Responsibilities were not few,
The pile got thicker as he grew,
Job, money, money, and job
A pressure of coming on the top

Like any other, his life got messed up
He felt he was all tangled up
For the money, the whole night he worked
Little dark circles and a hot coffee cup!

Marriage, kids, schooling, and relationship
Exhausted! He wished for a relaxing trip
His life runs faster than a metro
But guess what? The world is said to grow,
grow and grow...!

The best part came with retirement
Just sit back home and relax
Pension came on time
But need possessions and again stress.

Lying on the hospital bed
With a mental disease overhead

He realized stress and strain is not what one should take
Now happy with the money which you made?

You know what his children realized,
When do they perform his last rites?
It was the biggest possession that they earned;
When the priest said... "For you are dust
and to dust, you shall return"

Aarushi Prabhakar
3/05/2019

Dr. Sood in DMC also asked to run a few tests which were already familiar to us like IBD, IBS but as usual, there were no signs in the results to make it prove. So, he recommended a few medicines which didn't show its effect to page the improvement in Aarushi's consistent diarrhea where her thrombosis was slowly becoming the biggest enemy due to less blood supply towards the liver via her portal vein, the liver started to shrink from one side which was a disastrous sign. Firstly, her right vein was affected with thrombosis and then the left one also started facing the same problem along with it. We were tired of hearing the word 'liver transplant'. We tried to reach out to another doctor who could tell us something instead of the word we were listening to since 2018; basically, it was the 'hope' we wanted for Aarushi and in the search for that part I took her to Chennai in March 2020 along with my brother.

Our ears got introduced to the name Dr. Mohd. Rela who is the best when it comes to liver. After booking an appointment, which was also a struggle, we finally reached him for hope and he was just the opposite of Dr. Gupta in the terms of behavior as well as the way of approach towards his work.

Dr. Gupta was aggressive and he used to work according to his gut feeling which was an impressive watch too whereas Dr. Rela was too composed and calm in nature as well as his nature also seemed to show an impact on his work ways. In his clinic, there were almost 10 doctors from every field like the pediatrician, surgeon, gastro specialist, nutritionist which appeared as an impressive team, and when a patient entered his clinic, the doors used to get closed for another entry inside. After Dr. Rela looked into Aarushi's profile, he wanted to have suggestions from everyone on his team about the patient's health condition.

He suggested that the solution is liver transplant only but before making it possible, she needed an impressive amount of nutrients inside her body to make her strong enough so that she could at least survive the procedure as she was consistently going through severe and many different provocative diseases. The reason behind wandering for a long time was her blood loss happening via her anus in the way like 'water runs'. There was one more difficulty she faced after the liver transplant was hemorrhoids (swollen and inflamed veins in the rectum and anus that cause discomfort and bleeding).

At the end of the day when the blood supply is poor a portal vein, it will create a pressure which will surely try to make its own way to come out. We used to think that something had ruptured inside her because of which the lower gastrointestinal part was bleeding but who can think negatively about their own child's condition? We were at the same place too and when we informed doctors at Max, Delhi about her bleeding, they started making a link with re-transplant of her liver. I had a feeling that if Aarushi's diet will be taken care of then it might cure her thrombosis problems as being on medicines for over months and intaking the chemicals via syringes, her diet headed in a bad condition where she couldn't eat anything for which she also had the reason like there was a possibility that her stomach might be shrinked due to less intake of food. She used to make her meals cooked for herself with such excitement in order to eat but all she could have was a small portion of it.

Dr. Rela mentioned it very clearly that we can't even make a cut over her body as even that will consume a good amount of time to heal it; re-transplant had no chance to become an option for her present health. In my knowledge, the case was being handled well as he kept us in the hospital for 15 days and then he himself asked us to search for another accommodation that was close as no one likes to stay in a hospital for a longer period of time, they also inserted a feeding tube to provide her with the proper nutrients.

We had a memorable time as well in Chennai, we used to visit beaches where she never hesitated to carry her feeding tube, and later with time, we also had the concern of covid as the pandemic was increasing anonymously around the globe. We were worried about the thought of what If we might be stuck in the same place? So, we portrayed our concern in front of Dr. Rela and he suggested the same which was to move from Chennai back to Dehradun and then come back after a month or two as no one knew what could have happened in the next moment or day.

We were told by Dr. Rela that for the next 5 years, complications will be present but instead of worrying about the facts, we will handle those complications medically without making any cuts over her body where the liver will stay fine which won't need any re-transplant. We got a little bit of satisfaction so we came back to Dehradun and till July, we were just feeding her with the tube itself. Then, the festival was approaching which was 'Rakhi' that happens to be in the month of August. We made the visit to Jalandhar on 4th August 2020 to celebrate the festival at her maternal grandparent's house.

She found a new flare in herself in these times. She started playing badminton with her dad. She started to record videos, write more, be more creative. Walk often and had a self belief that she'll recover for sure. She even started the baking classes and even the dance. Doctor had suggested that physical activities are must for her. And now with her own self belief, she was totally into being more physically active. In her diary too, she has mentioned this part where her new flare towards healing could be seen.

The celebration was on peak, everyone was having a good time filled with all the happiness and why not to be celebrating when the whole family comes together! But later at night, Aarushi again had the motion full of blood, when I made a call to Dr. Shaleen at Max. He suggested that we admit her the next day as they were suspecting that she might have internal bleeding. They informed me about the planning of her surgery of portal vein bypass which will allow the blood to flow from another vein after the connection. We agreed with the thought as again it was a ray of hope to cure her problem of PVT; struggling from 3 years on and off-scale with some other medical problems in addition.

We took her to Delhi on 14th August 2020 for the portal vein bypass and then the next struggle was to arrange the graft which was meant to work as a vein. The doctor mentioned that they didn't want to use the rubber graft and Aarushi's body doesn't have anything like the requirement. So, they wanted to wait till the time the graft wouldn't be arranged from someone else's body (while going through the liver operation). We asked to leave as it would be a waste of time to wait in the hospital.

We got a call by 23rd of August to inform us about the successful arrangement of the graft and we reached back to Delhi on 26th August. On the 27th of August, she went through the surgery of portal vein bypass. We were being informed with the details that the surgery won't last more than 4 to 5 hours as well as the critical surgery, in the starting I had an assumption that it won't be equivalent to the liver transplant but when I had a word with an assistant of Dr. Gupta, my mind got the clarification about the risks and how big the surgery was! I called Aakash to come from Dehradun as it was something I couldn't handle by myself. Before the surgery, I dressed my daughter properly and told her that 'Aarushi, this will be the last time you will be going through the surgery and when you will wake up,

I will be standing right next to you, where all of your problems will be gone as well.

My daughter was positive enough and ready to go under the procedure which was planned for her. The surgery started and till afternoon we had no information about what was going inside the operation theater. In the meantime a nurse came outside, we asked her to provide us with some information and she just said, 'There were complications but everything is under control'.

On 27th August, the operation got over by 6:30 pm and not even a single doctor came to meet us. I got the text from Dr. Shaleen regarding the surgery which went fine and Aarushi will be shifted soon from the OT to ICU but we didn't hear anything from Dr. Gupta. Ritish texted after an hour to Dr. Gupta about the shifting process of Aarushi, he then reverted back saying she has been shifted and we could see her. After the surgery on the 29th, her creatinine, blood urea, as well as her liver enzymes, were increased but we were informed that it will be happening due to the surgery and with time, it will come down to a normal level but it didn't happen. Her body started deteriorating; the platelets count was getting low and her whole body got covered with the red spots.

On 3rd September, she was again shifted from the ICU to the private room and my daughter kept telling me that she doesn't want to stay inside the ICU or in the hospital anymore and that she wanted to go home. She said the line out loud that she knows 'Nothing can be done to cure me, just take me home and I will be fine.' Somehow, we convinced our child to stay without knowing about the upcoming complications and one thing which was noticeable, was whenever she used to come back from the procedures, the energy used to be on the next level inside her nerves, talking without getting a stop, asking for her phone to make videos and ordering good food for someone else as she loved to browse new dishes.

These were the general Aarushi's reactions and I am mentioning every bit of it because this time when she came back from the surgery, she was quiet, wanted to sleep all time, didn't want to talk to anyone, covering herself with the blanket till face like she was upset about something or angry with someone. We all thought that it must be happening because of the healing process or exertion under her skin due to the major surgery.

Around 8 pm, after she was shifted from the ICU, Aarushi had upper gastrointestinal bleeding where she vomited just blood which was horrifying for me to see her in the condition. The moment she vomited, her face looked like she had made a big mistake or a feeling where she knew that her condition won't be able to cope this time. Again, she was shifted inside the ICU for her further monitoring. She was feeling discomfort from the inside, all those reactions were not her mood swings but I think it was some medical discomfort she was experiencing.

Her body couldn't handle the pressure which was created inside of her system via internal bleeding which might be caused due to the rupture of any area involved in the portal vein bypass and at that time, my brain was working in a direction that couldn't think of the possibilities of things the way we planned, might head wrong as we were still running upside down in the hospital with the feeling of hope and not even a single person ever mentioned or said anything regarding the idea was wrong itself.

After the bleeding happened, she was taken to the fourth floor, and instead of shifting her inside the ICU, the suggestion came to take her inside the bigger room which was present in front of the ICU. The episodes of vomiting the blood got even more frequent where her mouth was showing severe infection like white greasy spots or fungus, it was declared as the reaction of medicines she was taking for a long time.

These lines are the toughest part to put into words as the description becomes the flashback which gets intense to move ahead but then I can't stop too! So, the coming days started getting critical for us but I didn't have any idea about the situations going over the path which was filled with the statement 'not coming back'.

A change felt by me which was showcased by Dr. Gupta; he was not too interested to know further information of Aarushi's condition as he was making rounds on the fourth floor, the same floor where Aarushi was also present but his attention was occupied by other patients even though my daughter was going through tremendous illness. And it's still a mystery why he had such an ignorant phase for us after the surgery! Suddenly Dr. Gupta entered as he wasn't aware of the fact that the room he was stepping in was Aarushi's but as he already entered, he started checking her vitals as well as the present condition where my daughter just quoted one line that

'Let me go home'

Dr. Gupta quoted that **'Who wants to stay willingly inside the hospital; once you are fine, I will discharge you'**

'No, I won't be fine I know! Just let me go home and I will be fine'

But every time she was vomiting it was nothing but blood coming out of the system and again, I want to ask if that was normal? On one side the blood was coming out and on one side the blood was dripping inside via cannula. It seemed like an internal haemorrhage but why wasn't it getting fixed? Why weren't getting any answers about what will happen next or why was it even happening? If the surgery went fine then why was the blood which was supposed to reach her liver coming out? They created a shunt between her portal vein and inferior vena cava to provide the blood supply to the liver but I guess it didn't happen exactly.

Dr Shaleen informed us that there's another patient in the hospital who has been declared brain dead. And if we talk to their family and if they agree, we can transplant their liver to Aarushi. As Aarushi's other organs were responding fine. Though the doctor said it'll not be a huge surgery, after going through the whole medical process so many times, now we knew it'll never be a small surgery. Neither in terms of risk nor in terms of the money. Retransplant was definitely a big risk and more than that, it would once again cost a lot. I remember Aakash immediately called a broker and was ready to sell his shop. There was no hesitation in his mind to even try this out. He didn't want even a single stone to be left unturned. Even if there was just a 5% outside chance of this transplant being successful, we were ready to try. We were ready to sell our soul and every inch of our body if required for our daughter's recovery. Although when Dr Gupta came for the round, he asked us to put these plans on hold. He said they will still have to keep Aarushi in observation for a few more days before thinking about another transplant.

I think Aakash knew in his subconscious mind that Aarushi's health is deteriorating more than we anticipated. It was a worrisome moment, but things were out of our hands. But these thoughts never popped into my mind. I have seen Aarushi fight since the day she was born, like the fighter she was. And I had a hope that she too, will fight again, and be better once again. But, as time passed by, she kept slipping out of my hands. She was tired; I could see it in her eyes.

Aarushi had so many plans for us and her future. She would always talk about them with a twinkle in her eyes. She once said, "Mumma, when I get older and get married, I will ask my husband to stay with us, here. Because I can't imagine and don't want to live without you." These things still linger in my mind; hoping they would come true. She also had big plans for our 25th anniversary!

She was a girl with so many hopes, dreams and ambitions in her life. A will to do something big, to create an impact on peoples' lives and to make the world a better place. But all the things were left unfulfilled. I lost everything that day. Time took her away too soon. Still, even after so long, I cannot accept what has happened. I still cannot wrap my mind around it. It doesn't feel real.

Each night, I go to her room to say good night and put a blanket on her bed. I believe she's still near me, looking at me with her beautiful eyes. I am always in turmoil because she's not with me and my belief is that she feels the same way. We couldn't be separated before, and we can't be separated now. Every morning, I go to her room to wake her up, talk to her because I know she is listening. Any and everything in her room is exactly how she left it, and it always will be as it is. I have cried, laughed, felt every emotion to feel her near me, whenever I hold the things that she loved. Whenever I touch her clothes, I know she's around and they smell just like her. She left her clothes, pictures, books, poems, all of her belongings; and ME. I will keep missing my Aashi until the day I join her and be reunited. Aarushi, you will be remembered just like your name, a ray of hope.

CHAPTER ELEVEN

Dad's Little Angel

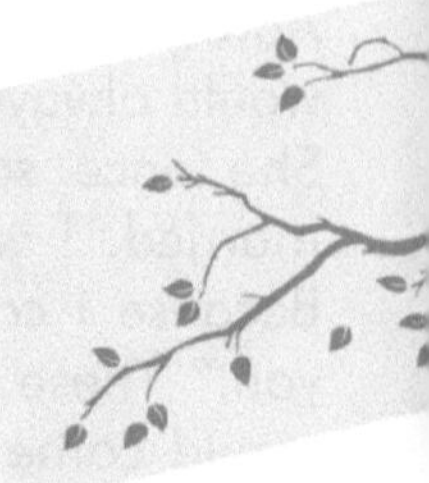

What Aarushi meant for Aakash is as difficult to put in words, as to explain the importance of a heartbeat for the human. There were no secrets in between them. To call them the support system of each other, will still be less accurate. To be honest, you could see that if one was going through the pain, the other could feel it without even uttering a single word.

Throughout the medical fight, we went through, or in fact, the Aarushi went through. Aakash stood with her like a pillar. If only someone could ever reinstate the confidence of healing in Aarushi, it was Aakash. And that belief brought up a calmness among the family. For Aarushi, Aakash was the saviour dressed as a knight.

I knew she understand relationships very well. She understands the importance of having someone who always has your back. She found her best friend in her dad.

"Relationships are not truly about being
someone's girlfriend or boyfriend.
It's about becoming best friends,
Who shares laughter and tears together,
Who act like parents and take care
of each other as siblings,
Who guide each other.
In short, it's all about becoming someone's true soulmate."

Aarushi

An instance I remember very clearly was the birthday week going on. Aarushi as usual was excited. But a little tragedy took place, as she forgot her mobile somewhere, or maybe it got stolen, but she was very tense and upset as she came home. I might have lost a little temperament for her to have misplaced her mobile and for being so careless. She was upset, apologetic, and in fact, worried that how will her father react to this.

I called Aakash for a little rain check, to update him with the situation so he doesn't burst out on her when he comes home. But as soon as Aakash heard about the incident, his first question was, "How's Aarushi? Is she fine? Is she upset? She didn't get hurt right? You didn't shout at her right?". And it was as sweet as surprising. He always had her back. When he came home he made sure to check on Aarushi and to cheer her up. Forgetting about the silly mistake, he made sure to comfort his daughter and he knew, it was her birthday week, her friends be posting all sorts of wishes and countdowns on social media, she wanted to be updated with that. Hence, she was very sad and not in a mood to feel any joy of her own birthday coming up. Aakash made sure not to let her feel down for even a second more. He made sure to cheer her up, to fill her with positive vibes. Aakash took her to shop immediately and got her a new mobile of the same brand. The mobile she lost was bought for her in August, on EMIs, now just after 5 months she has lost it, even the EMIs had not concluded yet. And Aakash didn't think twice before buying a new one, of the same brand and cost, once again on EMIs with the previous one's still to be paid, just for her one smile. She was thrilled to have the new mobile. Of course. That can sum up their relationship pretty well.

I think Aarushi found her hopes within her father, always. If I could say that they were mirror copies of one another, I wouldn't be lying about it. Both held courage as their topmost priority. Through the sick days, they both used to utter that this is nothing, it's just a phase, we'll get alright very soon. In those days, if you met Aakash, his confidence about the situation and positivity throughout the tough times reflected as it is on the Aarushi. Her self belief towards healing was all a happy result of the positivity that Aakash maintained around her. Aarushi also wrote some beautiful heartfelt lines for him.

DEAR DADDY

Sometimes I might be rude to you
Sometimes I may not talk to you
Sometimes you may feel I don't love you
But daddy, not loving you can't be true!

Aarushi Bhakar is what you call
You take care of me as I did of my doll
The shoulder rides from place to place
Gave a big smile on my face

Just one wish and you never failed to complete
Thanks for all the long drives we enjoyed on the car's backseat
I promise I'll one day make your name shine
I am glad daddy that you are mine.

You have always stood by my side
And held my little hands
I still have to learn a lot from you
The things I don't understand

I just wish when you blow the candles today,
That God fills your life with happiness every day
I love you daddy and I'll always do
Only this what was left to say.

Aarushi Prabhakar
14/05/2020

It was daddy's special, special bond that was described by her in a beautiful manner. Aakash was her 'genie', a magical person who would do anything to make her wish come true. What a strong person he is! He wasn't just there for her but always signified his presence like a tough pole in my life and I am blessed that still, he stood by my side because of whom I get the strength to move forward.

One another thing that shows the attachment of the bond that they two held is that Aakash changed his lifestyle for her. More so because of various superstitions, he had made in his mind because of Aarushi's deteriorating health. But still, it was out of hope and concern. Aakash builds up the superstition that whenever he eats eggs, Aarushi falls sick. Hence, he completely quit egg. He assigned a specific colour to each day of the week, for good luck and started wearing clothes of the same colour on the designated day.

Aarushi was a giggly child. Always smiling, always happy. Even when she was in pain she would smile and try to comfort me instead that it's nothing, she ain't feeling pain, she'll be alright, no need to worry. But it was tough for me to unsee the reality, to ignore her pain that was visible through her strong smile. And at the same time, when you would look at Aakash, her father, he would feel the same pain and he'll also hide it behind that big wide smile to comfort his daughter and me. He would utter the same things, that it's just a phase and she'll be alright, she's strong, it's nothing, just a temporary situation. And that's why I said, they were exactly the mirror copies of one another. They were exactly the father-daughter duo that we read in stories.

CHAPTER TWELVE

Family!

Of course! Mentioning her grandparents is something that meant a lot for her. She was a lovable child and everyone always seemed like they meant to love her. Grandparents are someone who just lives their own kid's childhood all over again by seeing their kids grow up in the same way.

MY GRANDPA

The day before I was born,
You were happy, excitedly waiting for tomorrow's morn!
A bit confused when I would be playing on your lap?
You always made sure that there was nothing which I could lack.

From my head to toe,
You made me strong,
As you're today,
And was before.

That evergreen smile on your face,
It made me confident and strong,
You were the one, who taught me,
The difference between right and wrong.

Oh! Confused? Whom am I talking about?
I'm a body and he is my soul
He is the one who would never leave me,
He supports me today and further
He is no one else,
He is my grandfather!

Aarushi Prabhakar
02/05/16

Aarushi considered family the most important element in her life. And not just with parents and grandparentsm but with everybody. She would always engage in interesting conversations with her cousins, have their back and always support them in all their endeverous. And her perspective on apologies was also wholesome. Her take on apologies could be clear from her little poetry:

You can't say SORRY,
Each and every time,
Because sometimes
' something hurts so badly
That a 'sorry',
Can't take away the pain.

Aarushi

We can understand from here that she understood the meaning of having each others back and there was no looking behind. One cannot just excuse themselves by saying a sorry, one has to commit to their actions within a family and hope that others will understand always. Because that's what families do, isn't it.

A SPECIAL BOND IN MY LIFE- MY MAMU

As you heard the girl's cries,
I am pretty sure your happiness touched the highest skies
You let your school bag remain far away
With your niece, you wanted to stay

Niece! Yes! A niece by relation!
But a daughter's connection
Our hearts are connected by the creator above!
I know for each other we can shower all our love.

Your love for me never changed!
It's the best relationship so far, I gained!
You never cared about your sleep your
work and your family life,
You are one of those people who helped me thrive!

Words are too little in the dictionary for you!
People like you are very few,
What would I do without you, I really have no clue,
But I just want to say I love you as much
as anyone can ever do.

Thank you for your endless love for me,
You not only took care of me,
But everyone else in the family
We all are thankful to you and I just pray to God
That he makes me at least a way like you!

You have to sun me on a cradle to now
I am sure you know me better than I know you somehow!
Sorry for the anger I may give you!
I will be better and you will see.
But mamu albumin is not my cup of tea.

Aarushi Prabhakar
10/01/2020

My brother Ritish did not just have a relationship of Mamu with her, but a strong bond of being best friends, who shared every little secret of their lives. All the gestures were the priority before anyone in his life and I don't know whether anyone else has experienced the same but he was like a second mother for her. He didn't even show his trust when it came to Aarushi's health conditions. He used to research her diseases or problems she had to go through where he used to answer all of us with the information. He had for our queries like he had completed his bachelorette in medicine. All the terms which we couldn't even spell or pronounce properly were known by him so while all the procedures Aarushi has been through were accompanied by Ritish. She had a belief that if my Mamu is here, I will be going out of the hospital alive as he was extra attentive. A bond which they did share was purely the best friends forever like,

Were always together,

Were one of a kind,

Three words describe them

"Partners In Crime"

And Ritish also wrote something beautiful for her to describe her

"Poem by Mamu for Aarushi"

What a splendid day it was
A beautiful girl was born.
Wrapped with God's love and blessings
She was just an angel's clone.

Living her life like a princess
She was surrounded by a demon,
Pushing all the troubles on the backfoot,
She asked for challenges to come on.

While fighting with the demon for a long,
She asked sorrows to hold on.
I have a lot to explore and write,
She asked life to move on.

One day God saw this little girl in trouble
He pushed away all the demons
Keeping his hand on her head,
He asked her happiness to turn on and on and on...

Aarushi – the light of my eyes

I miss her more than I can comprehend in words.

My heart used to beat for her, without her the rhythm of my heartbeat is missing.

The world can never be the same for me again, a void that is created cannot be fulfilled

The more I think of her the more I feel the pain, it is emotionally draining to revisit the memories and put in words

But let this be about Aarushi and not anyone else.

From my lap to the Hospital bed, it has been a comprehensively short but most memorable journey that I can ever remember.

She has been more of a motivation towards the people around her, especially me. Just as her name Aarushi- the dawn, she was the light of the day, sunshine for the people around her. I still remember as she was administered Ryles tube, she kept the taste buds alive by opening a foodie channel on youtube. That's the persistence that one has to keep alive in himself- no matter what the situation is you can still keep yourself in your mind.

An analogy for the people who missed being in the company- you only live a moment in time. **She was the real Anand- the vintage movie, where reel role was played by great Rajesh Khanna who knew the end was near but was never perturbed by the thought of it.** From reel to real life- she was the pinnacle of confidence and motivation that one can derive inspiration from. Her charm never faded regardless of any situation that came in front of her.

Aarushi, you are the light of my eyes and
sight that I shall always miss.

Love you lots- I know you are in a better world and would keep the surroundings alive with your vibrance.

-by Sachin

She loved her family; it was the priority of her life to move forward by taking her family with herself. She didn't have any successful thoughts just for herself but she wanted her cousins to accompany her with the same. The dinner should be served while every single person be sitting together, basically the same dialogue I would use which confronted her views was

Family is that eats together, lives together and stays together.

CHAPTER THIRTEEN

Positives V/S Negatives

Positives and negatives are the two features of life,
How you deal with them
It's totally your choice
Positives would keep you elated and strong
Negatives will transfer cries and wrongs
Love, laughter, and peace
Would fill your heart with memories
Sorrow, cries, and depression
Would just give worries and tension
One should never let negatives take over
One should never get frightened in any phase of life
With smile, happiness, and positivity,
One can always strive
Keep your spirit positive and high
That is the plane to the vast sky
Negative will make your life gloomy and dark
But what's more important is a positive spark
Just smile and laugh till stomach aches
And let not the positive vibes in you ever break

Aarushi Prabhakar
28th June 2019

Although I have said that this would be really close to my heart. But honestly, I don't know what I am up to today and what I want to say. Words feel like they have got locked in some corner of my heart because only my heart goes what I won't tell to this little place known as 'planet earth'.

I just want to try and change the perception of people on my things- to start with I will talk about the word "suffering". Suffering according to the Oxford dictionary means "to be badly affected by a disease, pain, sadness, stress or hardship!" If you feel that you are suffering or God is making you suffer, you yourself become intensively weak, to some extent I will say further may sound ill-logical and to some who has the courage to find light in the darkness, it may sound positive!

The word "suffering" is created by any other person like you and me! People believe that God is making us suffer-look how happy the other people are, to them he hasn't given any suffering! For us now suffering means a price for a hard time. Now for a moment believe that this world is created by the supreme being and its meaning is a challenge! And he only chooses those people for these challenges who are courageous and brave. If any of my audience is listening to me and thinks he is in pain-just repeat after me! I am courageous, brave and I accept this challenge and I will win!!

I myself have seen a lot of ups and downs in my life, many challenges, many hospitals, many tears, many procedures of stress! I too, used to think why me? But now I know me! Because I am brave and I am a fighter. Don't blame others for what you are going through today, you get what is served by destiny! Just look now! China-the epicenter of CORONAVIRUS is back to its normal life while the entire world is suffering.

A teacher, staff members, and other employees are getting salaries-although they must not be seeing a very-very bad stage, I meant almost many of them but a daily wager- who made the house we are in right now- 'safe', have to sleep hungry. But amongst all such things, he still goes to get food to feed his children with hope and positivity. No matter what you go through, positivity is very important. Carrying a positive attitude is like carrying a candle on a dark road and it has the capability of changing your life completely by never sending smiles, the laughter of brightness.

23rd April 2020

The whole world started taking the word "Karma" so much with so many cases of power and anger in its eyes. Walking around, everyone cursed people who have hurt them. "You will face Karma". Today, I am standing on my balcony and I can't hear anyone. There is complete silence, just the drops of rain are talking today! Such lovely weather and I realize, when today no person can be seen on the road, all are facing karma. Even kept animals in cages, locked. Today, we are locked – karma

#lockdown

#corona

26th April 2020

Look to the skies

And the

Stars will guide you.

Look to your heart

And you will

Always know the way.

[*the above articles of this chapter were written by Aarushi].

How can someone write this so maturely! This will always be a question of mine to her. I have no idea how someone can be so wonderful when it comes to expressing not just their emotions but also whatever was happening outside her thoughts. The world was "suffering" but she knew the cause and named it "karma". Let's talk about something, parts of her which were her achievement through which she knew who she was

CHAPTER FOURTEEN

The Bonus Days

After the end of her glory days in school, a new journey has to begin which is not just a dream to live your life in your own conditions but also to learn more about life as you get out in the real world by leaving your comfort zone, your shelter behind; you enter into 'the learning process.'

I wanted Aarushi to stay at Dehradun itself for her further studies but she didn't agree with me, her dreams were different and of course bigger than what I wanted for her! In the first place she wanted to go to Delhi for the college but we couldn't agree as there was no one to provide help at instant so, the next option sounded more righteous which was Jalandhar where she wanted her admission at Lovely Professional University, Punjab but again my mind wasn't allowing me to see through her eyes of shine that how important it was for her! Again, I was all worried about how she will manage to live without me? How would she take care of herself regarding food or taking medicines on time or any other work where she might feel difficult to do? I couldn't see her managing all the obstacles altogether.

My parents are settled in Jalandhar so they made me feel confident that she will be taken care of in a proper way without any neglect. Ritish also agreed where his wife supported the whole discussion too about managing everything with Aarushi. Finally, I made up my mind to let her live the bonus days. The admission was done and she was ready to take her place as a student of English

Honors, the campus was good as well. We also gave our visit to the head of the English department where my daughter told him all about her poems and writing habits regarding the topic, she felt like giving the thought about it.

Everything was going fine, I was happy with the satisfaction for my angel's future and as she had to join the college from the first week of August so here comes her shopping importance for her new place to walk in. She was on the seventh cloud to join her college but I was feeling a bit low from inside and maybe it was just one of the demerits of being a mother you all could name it. A feeling of accepting the reality when your child will no longer live under your roof is discomforting.

From the first week of August she started her college and my brother used to drop him regularly. After my brother drop her at the college, she used to make a video call to me to show herself how pretty she looked every day and especially her first day as it was so satisfying to see her grinning as well as shining but those days didn't last for long because Aarushi again got sick after 15 to 20 days of her college. She had to come back to Dehradun and immediately, we had to take her to Delhi which has become a saddening part for her as well, because it wasn't going to be the routine check-up but she was hospitalized again in August 2019.

Then we took a decision that it won't be any harm if she will drop the year and stay with us in Dehradun and join back in the coming next year once she will be back at her strength completely; though she dropped the year in spite of sitting on the bed all day, she joined baking classes and started investing her time by making some delicious food and baking. It would be unfair if I won't say that her dishes used to be mouth-watering. She learned to bake delicious cakes, muffins, pastries, pies, etc.

In 2020, I suggested she get admission in English Hons. from the Doon University in Dehradun but the last date to submit the form was 30th August. She took all her certificates to Delhi along with her while she was heading for her surgery as planned so that she may apply for it from there itself. On 30th August, she informed Aakash about her plan of submitting the form for Doon University and she made sure that her father should complete all the columns needed to be filled. Besides bearing the horrific pain, she got up to get her photograph done for the form with a sweet smile and after the submission of the form, **it got accepted.**

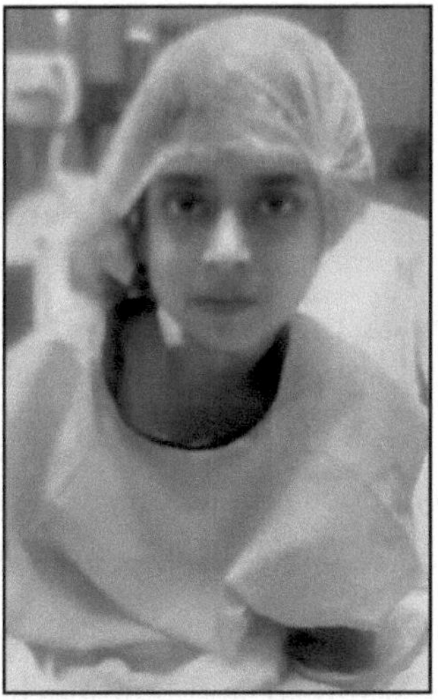

Aarushi also made an account on Youtube.com with the name **'FOODGENIC'** where she dreamed of having the silver play button. It's a humble request to the readers to subscribe to her channel as I still want to fulfill her dreams because I can't stop believing that she doesn't live with me anymore, she is not visible to our naked eyes but I feel her inside me; my is daughter still alive within me and maybe your one subscription could help her fallen dreams to reattach again by getting that silver play button for her.

THE LAST POEM

(FOR HER VICE PRINCIPAL, MICHELLE GARDNER)

Enchanting eyes, blooming face,
Mistress, who works with all the grace!
Just like a candle,
That gives us light
Never failing to fulfill all the responsibilities
She works day and night!

Destiny made us all stay away!
"Loss of children?" No way!
A woman who is independent, hardworking,
opinionated, and unique,
She made the youngsters learn, even
at the time of pandemic peak.

Nothing in the world is completely flawless,
Except for your ideas and thoughts that are truly priceless!
Today may the winds of heaven blow and whisper in your ear!
That how special you are and how much you are dear!

Wish you a birthday that you will never forget,
A day packed with pleasure,
Your very best birthday yet!

And when your birthday is over,
After you spent it merely,
I pray that happiness, joy, and fun,
Fills your birthday yearly.

-Aarushi Prabhakar

16/08/2020

And that was it, it was her last poem, her last blow of thoughts, her last writing which she always loved doing and I wish I still could have her more writings where I would be able to sit and watch her writing; I also know that it's impossible in this life I am breathing now but in the next life she will be surely coming to me only as I still have a hope to meet her again.

CHAPTER FIFTEEN

Unheard Emotions

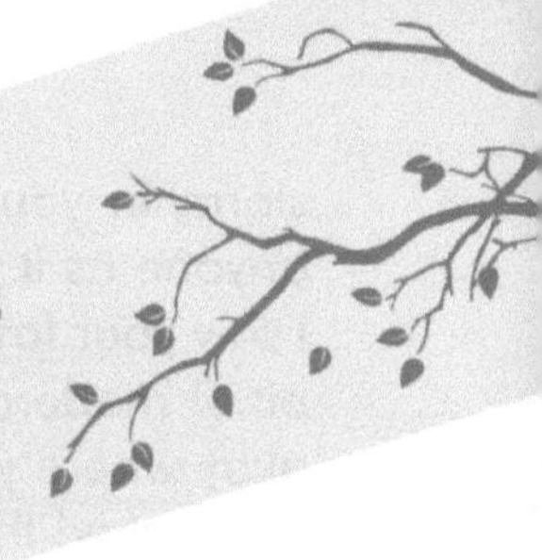

When the magic of my life, soul that held me together and the hope of existence- my daughter left this world, I started writing diary just like she used to. And I feel, these excerpts from my diary are necessary for you all to catch the understanding of my heart and mind in depth. You'll realise that I have placed my heart naked open in the plate for you all. You consume it, as it may please you.

27th August 2021,

Today, I won't ask my child how are you because I know how much pain you are bearing every second, how depressed and scared you are as you have to go inside the operation theater. I am recalling the incident when you had to undergo your big surgery. An aunty working in the hospital came to make sure that you are clean and ready for the procedure, do you remember Aashu? But your face looked as long as a fiddle while bathing and getting ready where you were handing me over your earrings as well as chain and I saw you crying! I asked you about the reason and you said,

'Mumma, I am scared! I don't know why?'

At that point in time, I answered with full confidence and relaxed nerves, 'There is nothing to worry about as it's just the matter of 2 to 3 hours of surgery and you will be healthy as a horse in some time' but seeing you cry made my heart start pondering too. It was 8 in the morning when they were taking you inside and I saw the terrifying storm in your eyes which was not being understood by anyone as it was an unheard storm enlarging inside you. I saw your favorite anesthetic doctor and I went into a little bit of moderation with the thinking that everything will be okay where your mamu (Ritish) also requested Dr. Gupta to proceed the surgery by himself but I had no idea that I should have buried that thought even before coming out.

And I had no idea that the dream I saw on the 25th night would be true!

"I saw the precisely similar event that came about for real on 27th which was Aarushi being taken inside the operation theater and instead of 2 to 3 hours, the doctors are taking prolonged time to finish the surgery and she is not coming out".

You know your mother very well that how worried I get when I stay away from you even if it's a matter of a few hours, the nightfall has started to take place in the sky where I couldn't hear anything about you. It was getting late to see you and as usual, my mind started becoming stretched over millions of thoughts; all I could be known with the fact that there was no news instead of monitoring or keeping under observation to see whether the shunt was properly showing its effects or not. The monitoring time was taking all of my patience away via my blood thinning in the affirmations about how you must be keeping inside Arshu? Then I heard a line **'She will be shifted in some time'** and it sometimes took place at 7 pm.

Later at 7 pm, we got informed that you are being shifted in the ICU where your father and mamu saw you outside as except me no one else was allowed to step inside the ICU room but seeing your consciousness, I was grinning in the hope that now everything will come back to normal, my Aashi was awake and you were being you Arshu. You started showing your stubbornness in order to ask for water but how could anyone provide your wish as you just came out of the long surgery where it was totally inhibited to do so, somehow after your continuous mulishness 'drop by drop' the water was being provided to you.

Two to three hours later, you were being shifted to a separate room inside the ICU. Without sleeping, I kept watching over your vitals and blood pressure with the fear that it's a critical night but I know you ordered the nurse to give you cold juice the moment you will be waking up in the morning and you got it!

On 9th September,

Hello Aarushi,

What am I supposed to write today, you only dictate me! For the last few days, I was just fighting with myself and now I understand why you kept saying 'No one means no one could ever understand what I have been through with the feeling of being sick where doctors opened me up and stitched my body all over again.' And after surgery every single day started becoming a struggle to go through as new problems kept standing in the way of the retirement of your health. I thought it would take 2 days in the ICU and you will be back but who knew that we had to stay till now. Jaundice was back along with the less urine output which meant by the doctors that your kidney is not working properly.

On 4th September, you went through your first dialysis because your urea, creatinine, and potassium level in the body was getting higher and not settling down. The local anesthesia was injected. I remember your childhood when you were getting pricked all over again which seemed to be like a block of wood getting perforated, layer by layer, in the search of your veins. The doctor informed us that only one dialysis would be needed to make all the imbalanced levels normal, after having the dialysis Arshu you were in a hyper mental state, like if you had the strength to remove all the tubes and walk out then I think you could have done it too.

On 5th September, there was no improvement in urine output and the lactate was 2.7 where the hemoglobin level was 7.2. Again, you vomited blood, where everyone was quoting as the infected fluid is coming out but I know my daughter was in severe pain and I don't even want to recall the feeling Aashi because I got weak! You tell me what else could I have done at that time? You kept telling me to take you home but see what I could do! Trying to cure you of something which couldn't be fixed afterward.

Even on 8th September, the condition was the same and just degrading as the time was passing where one more dialysis was already planned by the doctors. I know I have taken you out from the hell every time and this time also Arshu, I have given you all the strength to save you from the pain, but I was helpless in the matter of fact that I was looking for the hope which resides in yourself to fight. Your head was supposed to stay lower than the machine else there you could have faced a clot in your brain but you were not listening to a single word; like how badly you might be feeling anxious where I even made it clear to slap you not to listen to keep your head down.

On 9th September morning, the dialysis was stopped as the clot generated which couldn't be any safer to proceed forward and after shifting in the front room of the ICU, the vomiting of blood happened again. It was not stopping and no one was doing anything about it. I was getting helpless as well as impatient for not taking any steps to stop the blood coming out via her vomit; I cleaned the vomit, changed the clothes then doctors finally planned to do her endoscopy to check from where she was bleeding internally so they could put the band in order to stop the complications.

You were asleep when doctors took you for the endoscopy, the eyes were closed! So, I thought it might be the weakness due to the dialysis. I did see Dr. Gupta went inside the room 'two times' but it was unbelievable as well as astonished to participate in an endoscopy procedure. I have never ever seen him before doing the part which made me ask myself a lot of unanswered questions. The moment you were being shifted back to the ICU room from endoscopy, the torment was unendurable to lie down where your hands were raised above to hold you in our arms.

The whole night she was just screaming her lungs out, it was terrifying to watch for anyone and I was the mother who had to see every part of it where the doctors asked to shift my daughter on a ventilator, gave us the clearance that it's just to support her system getting stressed and the next day, she will be fine but it never happened. The 'fine' part didn't visit us this time as after putting her on the ventilator she had to go through the third dialysis for 24 hours which was risky. Dr. Shaleen also came on the rounds where he just used a statement to hate him enough for life,

'Ma'am, maybe she will not survive.'

The whole night was spent in shedding tears when I went to see her inside the ICU at midnight but still, I have no idea why I left the room after only a few minutes! What was going inside my mind? Maybe I had no strength left to see her in the condition she was and my eyes were continuously plunged over the door of the ICU room.

"On the 12th night also, I had another dream which was seeing my maternal grandparents (my Nani and Nana)

and they were looking at me and smiling like they wanted to give an assurance of something which I couldn't understand" but I understood later.

On 13th September 2021,

By 5:30 in the morning, we were called inside the ICU to tell us the news which I still couldn't be able to accept. Doctors said that 'She has been provided with a high dose of medicines to which she has stopped responding now' and my Arshu was too quiet, her eyes were stuck with the tape to close; I can't forget her face. I was sitting with her from 7 am, gently putting my hands over her skin, was kissing her hands then her face and kept telling her that please Arshu don't leave me because **'Your mother won't be able to live without you'** but I guess I wasn't loud enough. She couldn't listen to my voice properly. I knew that my daughter was someone who could not even imagine staying without me so I had a feeling that she didn't listen to my voice, as the time was passing her heartbeat, as well as her blood pressure, was going down. What her soul might be dictating Aarushi while leaving me and this world?

By 4 pm she left the world and left me crying in front of her but 'I felt like she was around me, telling me to stop her'.

I wasn't screaming or weeping thunderously when I solicited everyone to do the same because I knew Arshu could observe me as well as other family members. I didn't want her to feel fearful after seeing us sobbing, she won't have scuffling to go wherever she is right now. We came back to Dehradun with Aarushi but this time she was not the same, there was a cold feeling, no one to jump around, no noises filled with sweetness.

Aakash rubbed her with some curd where I wrapped her around with a beautiful red suit after washing her hair; the last parcel she ordered was a 'purple kurta' and I set down that with her only as it was raining heavily on that day so, I thought if her clothes will get dampened, at least she would acquire one more piece of cloth to commute. Aashi was going where I felt helpless because even after wanting her to cease with me, I had to let her go.

I will not fear the end,
Or that I will die alone,
The day I lost my child,
All I feared was gone.

I will not take my life,
But I am not afraid to die,
The day I lost my Aashi,
All my fears said goodbye.

Do not fear my death,
Through tears I know you will cry,
I will be at peace at last,
Beside my angel in the sky.

These lines portray the end feelings of mine, which I get every single day since the day she has left me all alone. I know one day; I will be meeting her at heaven's gate but till then I just want her to take care of herself.

I am just breathing like a machine; I have stopped remembering things as well because all I can think of is her. I can't let the feeling or the belief go away from her presence, as the soul residing inside my body has left with her, she was the light of my day. So, could anyone tell me how to feel alive after giving your soul, your reason to smile, feeling of warmth or should I quote 'everything'!

A year has passed, but I still haven't come to terms with accepting reality. Aarushi come back, as I have still not given up on you and I know you must be hearing my thoughts as well as watching your Mumma crying alone.

You asked me to write like you loved to portray your feelings in words, see I have finally written something I had inside me for a long; **Aarushi (a ray of light)** this is for you and I hope you will love it.

-Shruti Prabhakar

Aarushi's Room

Printed by Libri Plureos GmbH in Hamburg, Germany